THE 4 PILLARS OF
SHAMANISM

| FOUNDATION | CONNECTION | JOURNEY | SPIRITS |

113 BEGINNER TECHNIQUES & INSIGHTS

to Harness Your Inner Power and Intuition With Shamanic Rituals. Find Balance, Harmony, and Healing by Connecting With Your Spirit Guides

INGRID CLARKE

Table of Contents

Introduction

Are you lost and seeking guidance to reconnect with the spiritual side of life? Captivated by shamanism but need help knowing where to begin? This book is the perfect source to help you understand one of the oldest practices that can provide healing on your journey. It contains the knowledge and understanding needed to help you progress.

Surrounded by the rigors of modern life, the impacts of physical and psychological stress plague us daily. To counter this, alternate options are necessary to reach a state of equilibrium. Shamanism provides a way to align with spiritual aspects of the cosmos, unlocking the power of guardian spirits for healing and understanding.

After personally experiencing burnout, I have been devoted to studying different healing practices and gathering insight from metaphysical techniques and occult customs around the world. As an empath, I aim to bring forth the knowledge and understanding gleaned from a lifetime of experiences and in-depth research to those seeking healing. Subsequently, I will introduce the four pillars of shamanism in this book and illustrate how they can shape your viewpoint on portals that connect to realms inhabited by benevolent spirits. Through it all, you will discover how to unlock your consciousness of the sacredness of nature, establish contact with those entities, and communicate with them for counsel and therapy.

In the initial three chapters, you will understand shamanism more deeply, including its history, convictions, and healing capabilities. Chapter four will closely examine the various entities you can associate with, and chapters five and six will investigate the shamanic passage and other realms. Finally, chapters seven and eight will go into further detail on how to travel through a shamanic journey to communicate with your spirit guides and gain wisdom for healing.

With this book, I discovered a clearer understanding of the spiritual dimensions around me and how to find balance. I was given tools to make it through difficult times and remained in harmony with this newfound knowledge. It changed my life for the better, and it can do the same for everyone who needs guidance. Through this book, you can achieve harmony and balance by directly connecting to the spiritual realm. You will find 113 techniques, tips, and strategies to connect with realms inhabited by benevolent spirits. It's peppered throughout the entire book and it's intentionally designed this way to serve as your guide along each step of the process. It will help guide you in unlocking your awareness of divine beings and connecting with them to gain their infinite power for healing, balance, and harmony.

Moreover, this book is designed to give you access to shamanism's secrets and provide an alternate outlook on life. By employing this ancient wisdom, you can activate your inner creativity and use it to bring about meaningful change in your life. With this knowledge, you can see your current struggles from a completely different perspective, aiding you in finding solutions.

Ergo, investigate and discover the shamanic path with this book. Each chapter contains steps and strategies to help you better understand the theories and techniques you can use to make your spiritual journey more fulfilling. Learn how to access the knowledge held by spirits so you can bring your life back into balance and joy with shamanic practice. Unlock the power of divine beings to help restore harmony in all aspects of your life.

Now, set out on an adventure where self-discovery awaits you. All that is required is a willingness to explore and an open heart. Embark on a wonder, magic, and healing journey with shamanic practice. Let the ancient knowledge from spirits guide you to a place of balance and harmony.

Pillar 1
Foundation

Welcome to the first pillar of shamanism, the foundation. Here we will delve into the fundamentals of this ancient spiritual practice, which has been a part of cultures around the world for millennia. The core belief of shamanism is that everything in the world has a spirit, and these spirits can be communicated with to seek guidance and healing. As we explore further, we will investigate the concept of the spirit world and the role of a shaman, who acts as an intermediary between physical and spiritual realms. Finally, we will discuss how shamanic healing can help individuals reach physical, emotional, and spiritual balance. Join us in uncovering the history and traditions surrounding this ancient practice.

1

Understanding Shamanism

For thousands of years, shamanism has been an integral part of spiritual practices worldwide. This practice involves a shift in consciousness and connecting with spirits and natural forces. Although historically associated with remote or indigenous communities, it is now also embraced by many other cultures. People from all backgrounds have come to understand its power in seeking emotional, physical, and spiritual transformation.

What is Shamanism?

In the spiritual discipline of shamanism, healing and spirit-world communication are practiced, as well as an altered state of consciousness or ASC. One may use techniques like drumming or chanting to achieve this altered state. Some rituals employ psychedelic plants or mushrooms to create a uniquely mind-altering experience, which should always be done cautiously. Through these practices, shamans strive to access deep spiritual knowledge and seek to understand the interconnectedness of all life.

The purpose of Shamanism is to assist people in connecting with their deeper selves and unlocking secret knowledge, such as past experiences, future occurrences, and even alternate realms, like heaven. Shamanic healing works on both the physical and spiritual aspects; it can address physical problems while simultaneously aiding in discovering peace within one's mind, making life's troubles more manageable.

To find out if you are a shaman, ask yourself specific questions. A 'yes' response to any of them might mean that you have been practicing shamanic techniques in your life, even unknowingly.

- Do you feel a special bond with animals, even your pets?
- Can you forge deep connections with people, family, and friends?
- Is using plants, herbs, and crystals an easy way for you to help others heal their physical and emotional ailments?

Did you know that contemporary shamans are still around? You could even have one living close to you. Healing is their specialty; these shamans exist across the West and other regions. What sets them apart from traditional shamans is that they employ modern Western medicine and psychology practices as the basis for their healing remedies. Yet, they still draw on many of the same techniques practiced by historical shamans, such as meditation or divination, to gain insight into your body, mind, and soul, which can assist with recovery.

The term 'shaman' originates from the Tungusic languages. As such, a shaman is a spiritual leader who uses their abilities to heal, divine, and connect with unseen realms. Today this practice can still be found among indigenous populations in Siberia, Canada, and other areas. By utilizing spiritual techniques, shamans bridge the gap between physical and nonphysical realities to benefit their communities.

Although shamanism is widely practiced today, its roots can be traced back to traditional Siberian culture. In Siberia, shamans were highly regarded for their ability to enter trance states and explore other worlds. Whenever someone needed healing or guidance from beyond our reality, these shamans were called upon to help. They assisted people transitioning through life-changing events like childbirth or marriage. Likewise, they helped hunters predict success when hunting animals of significance to their tribes, such as bears

However, shamanism is not a religion but an ancient form of spirituality. Paganism, on the other hand, encompasses many different religious beliefs. Unlike the latter, shamanism does not require specific deities or beliefs about them; all it needs is someone with a passion for connecting with their inner self and the natural world. It has been practiced by people from various cultures around the globe, and anyone can participate if they are willing to put in the effort.

Despite common misconceptions, shamans and those practicing witchcraft do not have a unified code of conduct, such as Christianity or Islam. Instead, they typically draw from several traditions to create their unique practice. Paganism and witchcraft are often used interchangeably when referring to this type of magic, yet the two terms have distinct meanings depending on which group uses them. Witches tend to be eclectic and take inspiration from multiple sources rather than adhering to one specific path.

Likewise, shamans are not here to cause harm. Instead, they aim to bring balance into the world through their knowledge, intuition, and healing abilities. Those who have had the experience of participating in a shamanic ceremony as a part of their spiritual practice know that shamans do not engage in any cruel practices; instead, they work with spirit guides that assist them in helping individuals deal with challenging times. Shamans have been around since antiquity and remain so today to provide guidance when needed.

Traditional and Contemporary Shamanism

Shamanism is a distinctive method of engaging with the world through an intimate relationship with nature and other entities. It is done by utilizing altered states of consciousness, usually aided by mind-expanding herbs like peyote. In this way, shamans can access spiritual forces and explore life's deepest questions, such as *'why are we here?'*. This ancient practice offers insight into living in harmony with the natural environment and its inhabitants while continuing to grow spiritually over time. Shamans can leverage their knowledge by connecting with otherworldly beings for rituals known as "soul retrievals," in which a soul that may be stuck somewhere needs saving before it can return to where it belongs.

Chanting and drumming are powerful tools for achieving a higher state of consciousness. These practices allow one to reach the deepest levels of the mind and experience an altered state. The rhythmic repetitions evoke a trance-like atmosphere, facilitating inner exploration. By engaging in this practice, one can delve into esoteric realms rarely accessed by the average person.

Acting as healers, teachers, seers, and leaders, shamans are an integral part of many communities. They serve as a bridge between people and the spirit world, a role that is often revered in Indigenous cultures. Shamanism exists in regions across the globe, from North and South America to Europe, Australia, Asia, and Africa, and is still practiced by non-indigenous populations too. Shamans are valued for their work on behalf of their community members and exemplify spiritual understanding throughout much of the world.

Throughout history, many tribes have deeply rooted traditions passed down orally from one generation to the next. Shamanism is alive today through these oral teachings brought forth in stories. For instance, shamanism has evolved to adapt to current circumstances. While traditional shamanism involves practices that originated in ancient times, modern-day shamanism incorporates new techniques and beliefs that reflect the world today.

Practitioners of contemporary shamanism incorporate various tools and techniques to connect with the natural world and spiritual beings. As such, they use guided meditations, visualization, and energy work. While some practitioners may incorporate traditional shamanic practices into their work, contemporary shamanism is often viewed as more accessible and open to interpretation. Likewise, rather than adhering to strict traditions, contemporary shamans focus on individual growth and fostering a connection with the divine. Modern shamans also work with people of different cultures and backgrounds, as they recognize that spirituality is a universal human experience.

One notable difference between traditional and contemporary shamanism is their spiritual approach. While traditional shamanism focuses on interacting with spiritual entities outside of oneself, contemporary shamanism centers on an individual's personal growth and development. Modern-day shamans may use shamanic techniques like journeying or deep meditation to gain insight, but the focus is often on self-discovery. Additionally, contemporary shamanism can be seen as a more individualistic practice. Meanwhile, traditional shamanism usually involves the entire community. However, traditional and contemporary shamanism share a common spiritual connection and healing goal, even if their methods and approaches differ.

Overall, shamans believe that all beings possess a spirit, from rocks and trees to animals. Through proper interaction with these spirits (i.e., oneness), you can use them to heal yourselves. Also, whether journeying through other dimensions or finding solace in a peaceful walk through nature, embracing shamanism brings your ancestors' practice full circle, connecting to the shamans of centuries past.

History

Shamanism is an ancient spiritual practice passed down from generation to generation. Originating in Siberia and eventually becoming famous worldwide, indigenous peoples have adopted its practices everywhere, from North and South America to Africa and Australia. The term "shaman" comes from the Tungus word "saman," which refers to a person who can enter a trance-like state and communicate with the spirit world. As one of the earliest societies to embrace shamanism, the Tungus people carried on their beliefs throughout Siberia. Today, it is still practiced by various indigenous groups in many corners of the globe.

In each culture, shamanism had fundamental characteristics shared across most shamanic traditions. Among these are the capacity to communicate with spiritual entities, entering a trance state or altered consciousness to access the spirit realm, and believing that all things in existence are linked. Shamans were held in high regard by their communities and relied upon for their insightful understanding of the spiritual world, healing physical and mental suffering, interpreting dreams, and connecting people with the divine. Every civilization has modified these practices to fit its distinct environment, but these common threads remain unchanged.

The ancient practice of shamanism was prevalent among hunter-gatherer societies that lived during prehistory before written records began. This primitive lifestyle relied heavily on the connection with nature; their rites and rituals were integral to this relationship. Shamans utilized various methods to reach a transfigured state and access the spiritual realm—drumming, singing, and consuming entheogenic substances. From here, they could access supernatural entities and capacities to receive healing, knowledge, and guidance.

Across the globe, numerous cultures have shamans. From Native American medicine men and medicine women to Australian Aboriginals' songmen, Norse pagans' völvas, African tribal healers invoking herbs and magic spells, and Japanese Buddhists practicing Shintoism through praying rituals instead of direct contact, all these people have unique methods to communicate with spirits. Shamans were also knowledgeable in the diverse art forms of music, dance, and storytelling, which they used to pass down knowledge and insights to their community. Furthermore, they were considered wise counselors, guiding those who requested their help. By utilizing these different expressions, shamans effectively expressed the wisdom they received from the spiritual realm.

In many ways, shamanism is seen as a predecessor to many aspects of modern life, from religion and science to medicine. By entering altered states of consciousness, shamans employed methods like those used in hypnosis and meditation today. Praying to and conversing with spiritual entities is a ritual in many religions, similar to divination. In terms of healing, natural remedies are comparable to herbal medicine, which is commonly used in modern medical settings.

As the interest in spiritual pursuits grows, shamanism has become increasingly popular. Modern shamans have adapted historical practices to suit their beliefs and customs, including new methods while respecting the tradition's heritage. Those looking for a healing, insight, or a closer relationship with the world can benefit from this ancient practice. Shamanism offers abundant knowledge that can be used to develop a greater understanding of oneself and one's environment.

Shamanism in Modern Times

In today's world, shamanism has become a means to comprehend better how human energy works in harmony with our environment. It is not simply about beating drums or dancing around a fire; instead, it is an approach to healing oneself and others by connecting to the universe. Shamanism enables us to access our inner self, the spiritual realm, nature, and even our forbearers. This life path provides us with perspective and connection that can be used for personal and collective well-being.

Moreover, the current shamanic practices help those suffering from physical and mental conditions, such as depression and anxiety. Rather than masking their emotions with medications that could cause lasting harm, these healers help their patients identify their feelings. To further this healing process, shamans often perform rituals like smudging, which is the burning of herbs, to purify an individual's energy field and reconnect them with their true selves. This ultimately allows them to free themselves from lingering feelings of distress, enabling a path forward without being held back.

Ergo, shamans are not a source of harm or involved in any brainwashing, superstitious practices, or sinister cults. Instead, the term 'shaman' is derived from a Tungusic language, including Evenki and Evenk, meaning 'healer.' This hints at their ability to heal through their practice and is closely linked with the spirits of nature. As one's energy and soul align more with nature and its many forces, they become increasingly capable of healing those around them.

Searching for a shaman is easier than ever. They come in an array of styles and are found across the globe. Yet, select one well-versed in your desired tradition and willing to guide you to get the best support and direction.

People have long looked to shamans for healing, and Native American practices are only one such tradition. Many different methods of shamanic rituals are available today. As such, there are solo sessions to group gatherings in physical or virtual spaces, at home, or while traveling. No matter the setting, these ceremonies offer an opportunity to tap into bottomless inner power reserves.

Thus, shamanism can help people in today's society in several ways. It can help people to understand their problems and find solutions for them. Shamanism can also help people to overcome their problems. In addition, shamanism is a powerful tool for establishing a connection with your inner self and the universe outside of you. Likewise, it can solve issues in your personal life or interpersonal relationships. However, as mentioned, there are many different types of shamanic practices. That said, find one that fits your beliefs and personality.

2

Shamanic Beliefs

As we explore the origins of shamanism, we must also comprehend their beliefs and what roles the shaman plays in them. An exploration into why such a journey is pursued is necessary to understand this ancient practice fully. We will embark on this endeavor to gain insight into the mysteries of shamanic ways.

Communicating with the Spirit World

The shaman is a spiritual practitioner who has been present in many indigenous cultures worldwide for thousands of years. At its core, shamanism is a belief system that is founded on the idea that everything is interconnected and that spiritual and physical realms are not separate from one another. In fact, the shaman believes that spirits are all around us and can be communicated with through shamanic practices.

As a bridge between the material and spiritual realms, the shaman is revered for their talent of communing with those from beyond. From departed ancestors to gods and goddesses, they are said to be capable of reaching out and conversing with the spirits that inhabit our world. Connecting with the life force of plants and animals can provide insight and aid in healing. Moreover, shamans have used various tools and techniques to communicate with the spirit world. These can include chanting, singing, drumming, and dancing. Some shamans use hallucinogenic plants or other substances to help them enter altered states of consciousness, which can facilitate communication with the spirit world.

One of the primary ways that the shaman communicates with the spirit world is through journeying. This technique involves the shaman entering a trance-like state and traveling to other worlds or realms. The shaman is said to be able to communicate with spirits and receive guidance from them while in this state. As such, journeying can be done in various ways, but one common technique is to use a drum or other rhythmic instrument to help the shaman enter a trance state. Typically, the shaman will sit or lie down and close their eyes, allowing the drum sound to guide them into an altered state of consciousness. Once in this state, the shaman can explore other realms and communicate with spirits.

Divination is another means through which shamans get in touch with the spirit realm. This practice involves using tools such as bones, cards, or other objects to gain insight into a situation or receive guidance from the spirit world. The shaman may ask a question and then use the tool to receive an answer from the spirits. Besides that, dreams can be more than just random incoherent images and plots. Shamans believe it is a doorway through which wise and powerful messages from the spirit world can be conveyed. According to them, dream interpretation can help provide insight into pressing matters or even give guidance from the spiritual realm.

Being in communion with the spiritual realm is a gift of the spirits. It is said that the otherworldly entities choose the shaman and must undergo a stringent, rigorous training regimen to hone their talent. Through this, they develop and refine their capability to communicate with those beyond our plane of existence.

The shaman is viewed as the one who heals and speaks with the spiritual world. Through connecting with spirits, they can help those needing physical healing. By working closely with a patient, they can be guided to find the source of their ailment and then speak with otherworldly entities on their behalf to facilitate healing. In certain cultures, shamans may be invoked for more than just medical purposes; they are seen as vessels to converse with spirits regarding hunting or agriculture and perform ceremonies marking life transitions such as birth, marriage, and death.

Treating Malevolent Spirit Sickness.

Shamans are incredibly talented spiritual healers who can bring peace and harmony to those suffering from malicious spirit activity. Illnesses caused by evil spirits are common and can often be traced back to their influence. With the help of a shaman, these influences can be alleviated, allowing peace of mind and improved health.

For instance, in the case of sickness related to malevolent spirits, the shaman is called to perform a cure. Once the source of illness has been uncovered, help is requested from the shaman. A ritual is conducted to drive away the evil spirit that has taken hold of your being. Rituals can be done solo or as part of a group, with incantations, charms, and spells used in harmony to cast out the evil force.

When shamans heal an illness, they consider various factors before selecting the best action. One such factor is the harm caused to the individual, the family, or the community. Suppose an individual is possessed by an evil spirit, leading to harm to their family and others close to them. In such a scenario, the shaman may conduct a community-wide ritual to eliminate negative forces, requiring the active participation of the entire community.

Moreover, this practice involves entering a trance-like state where the shaman can communicate with spirits and send them away. In this state of spiritual communication, the shaman can request an explanation from the spirit as to why it is causing harm to its host if a problem has been left unresolved between them. For example, if the patient committed a misdeed, the issue can be settled before directing any negative energy away from the body.

Furthermore, shamans can create talismans that help ward off harmful spirits from their patients. The process of making these protective amulets involves the use of raw materials imbued with spiritual energy. Usually, a talisman made from bone or animal fur can serve as a conduit for the shaman's power, helping to keep negative energy away from the patient. Once complete, the affected individual can wear or carry the talismans to provide continued protection.

Besides that, shamans may use natural remedies to strengthen the body and prevent future malicious attacks by spirits. Prescribed remedies such as herbs, potions, and spiritual items are designed to support the immune system and restore balance to the patient's spiritual and physical well-being. Herbs, for instance, may be used to cleanse the body and spirit, purify the mind, and strengthen the body's defense mechanisms against future negative energy. Meanwhile, potions can dispel negative spirits and repel future spiritual attacks.

Shamans possess extraordinary spiritual healing skills to alleviate illnesses caused by evil spirits. These malevolent entities can be identified and exorcized using a range of rituals, incantations, and spells. By communicating with spirits in a trance-like state, shamans can remove negative energy and restore health to people suffering from malevolent spirit activity.

Vision Quests

A vision quest can be a powerful way for shamans to gain insight and wisdom from the spirit world. It is an immersive form of meditation, allowing them to tap into unseen realms, receive visions, and gain advice from supernatural entities. Different cultures and shamanic traditions offer varied approaches to the quest, each taking the participants on a unique journey of introspection and enlightenment.

To induce a trance-like state, shamans in some cultures ingest psychedelics or other substances. For others, they must fast and meditate over several days, readying their physical and mental selves for the voyage into the spiritual realm. With preparation completed, they embark on a journey of discovery, pushing the boundaries of what is real and what lies beyond.

Guided by the beat of a drum, shamans embark on a journey into the spirit world, where they encounter various spirits and entities that offer them wisdom and guidance. These ethereal beings may appear as animals, plants, ancestors, or mythical creatures. During this vision quest, the shaman receives messages through visions, sounds, and sensations that provide insight into their lives or what can be done to help others. For instance, these insights may include knowledge about healing rituals, divination techniques, and other spiritual practices. All these teachings aim to empower people with the power of nature and connection to one's inner self.

Hence, the vision quest is an essential part of shamanic practice because it allows the shaman to connect with the spirits and gain knowledge and wisdom that they can use to help others. By going on a vision quest, the shaman can gain insight into the spiritual world and bring that knowledge back to the physical world to help those in need.

Aside from that, the vision quest is a significant and profound experience for shamans. It is an opportunity to confront fears, gain an understanding of oneself, and uncover one's true path in life. This spiritual practice requires preparation, training, and guidance from a knowledgeable shaman. As such, it should not be undertaken lightly or without careful planning. Likewise, through the journey into the spirit world, the shaman can connect with their ancestors and cultural heritage. The power of this ritual makes it essential to consider all the risks involved and to enter it with intentionality and respect.

Shamanic traditions demand much of their practitioners; after years of study and practice, a vision quest can be embarked upon. For the journey to be safe and successful, the shaman must learn to enter a trance state, protect themselves from evil forces, and foster a profound connection with their spirit guides to communicate effectively.

Entering Supernatural World for Answers

Shamanic journeying is a spiritual practice that shamans of the past used to communicate with spirits. Today, it is still widely used by practitioners of many cultures across the globe. Also known as power retrieval, it requires entering into an altered state of consciousness with the help of tools such as drumming, rattling, and chanting. This journey has many emotional and physical benefits, such as healing, connection with the greater universal cycle of life and death, and connectedness with the natural world. It can be a profoundly transformational experience that brings guidance and understanding beyond our own.

However, shamanic journeys are not just a tradition of ancient cultures but are also part of modern life. People looking for guidance on their journey can contact a shamanic practitioner. For those with the will, plenty of techniques like guided visualization or meditation can be used to pursue this path independently. Whatever approach is taken, these journeys offer exciting opportunities to explore the unknown and gain valuable insight into oneself.

On the shamanic journey, shamans enter an altered state of consciousness and travel through the different levels of existence to find the missing power stolen by evil spirits. To achieve this, shamans usually use drumming to help them enter the altered state. Once they have reached the altered state of consciousness, they can travel anywhere in the supernatural world and communicate with spirits without physical bodies.

To begin this journey, a shaman must traverse the space between heaven and Earth to pinpoint the location of spiritual entities. Once this is accomplished, they must use cunning and wit to outplay them in a battle of wills. Doing so can enable them to reclaim the power previously taken from them. Not only are shamans adept at uncovering answers for others, but they also serve as conduits between us and the spiritual realm.

As such, shamans can travel to the supernatural world in search of solutions for those burdened by an evil spirit or ailment. To heal the sick, a shaman enters into a trance while clutching onto the hands of the affected individual, who soon follow their lead. In this altered state of consciousness, they may be able to uncover the past lives of both themselves and their patient. Likewise, shamans can comprehend where their souls have journeyed post-death if reincarnation is believed. This method is called 'scrying' and utilizes mirrors or other reflective surfaces to serve as gateways into another realm that holds answers to questions posed. Through scrying, shamans can find and diagnose the fundamental cause of a disease or issue, granting direction and healing.

Evoking Animal Images as Spirit Guides

Shamans are powerful spiritual guides who use their talents to help others. With the ability to shape-shift into different spirits and creatures, they are known for their close connection with animal companions. Such mystical bonds guide healing rituals, connecting the physical and spiritual realms.

As spiritual intermediaries, shamans can tap into the power of animals through spirit journeying. They are messengers who can switch between different forms in this world or the next. Shamans serve as guides and healers, bridging the divide between physical reality and divine realms. By invoking images of animals, they can access a pearl of higher wisdom and help us progress on our spiritual journey.

In traditional cultures, the shaman embodies the three facets of existence—past, present, and future. They are a healer who can see into their patients' bodies and souls, psychopomps guiding souls through death and rebirth, and an instructor teaching people how to live in harmony with their environment and each other. This connection allows them to traverse all worlds: the living world with its flora and fauna, the mortal world where our ancestors remain, and even more distant realms such as heaven or hell if those exist within your culture.

Having an "animal helper," such as a spirit animal, is the key to traversing alternate dimensions. If you find yourself in bed, feeling ill one day and then the next morning experiencing some relief yet still feeling exhausted due to your sickness, it could be a sign that something or someone has visited while you were sleeping. These spiritual forces can take many forms and offer unique insights into our realities.

By using rattles, drums, and other instruments, shamans can access the spiritual realms and call upon the animal spirits. Through the power of song or chant, they can bridge worlds and open up new horizons to explore. Different cultures have crafted various tools for such expeditions, ranging from gourds to seashells or metal bells. Native Americans often employ gourds for their rattle, making needs, yet these days some shamans opt for more modern material, like metal gourds, that can just as quickly help them on their journey.

As the shaman calls forth omens or spirit guides in the form of animal images that show up on amulets and drums, these symbols reflect the shaman and their patient. Such an image may be of a real animal, but it can also represent something beyond what we know about physical creatures. For instance, if one witnessed an eagle flying over their house during the night, followed by a dream of being chased by that same bird, this could point to a person facing specific difficulties and requiring moral support. The eagle would symbolize this person's struggle, but eagles are also renowned for their strength; they can fly high above any hindrance without requiring external support, insinuating that they will overcome any problem without relying on anyone else.

Thus, a shaman may use the form of an animal totem as a spiritual guide to give initiates power over their destinies. It can also symbolize you and your life's journey, which holds special meanings or shows significance. Animal totems can act as guardians, protectors, or even counselors on the journey to understanding yourself and the world around you.

Yet, shamanism is far more than just the practices and rituals of shamans. Through their work, healing abilities, and hunting prowess, animals in spirit form often aid them. Stories have been told of shamans transforming into animals to commune with their animal guides or using an animal's behavior as a sign from the gods that someone needs a particular cure or remedy. This special connection between shaman and beast can create powerful transformations and healing moments.

Performing Divination

Other forms of divination, including scrying, throwing bones or runes, and predicting the future, can also be done by a shaman. They can then give you advice and insight into what the future may hold by doing this.

Shamanic bones, taken from animals such as leg bones or ribs, have long been used by shamans for divination. The bones are thrown into the air or cast onto the ground. Depending on how they land, shamans interpret this as an omen to determine what may be coming up in their lives, as well as that of their clients. With this method of divination, shamans hope to gain insight and answers to their questions.

Runes are an ancient method of divination used by shamans, which can influence events in a person's life. Carved on pieces of wood or stone, they were traditionally used to record information like clan lineage and property ownership. Today, these symbols are still popularly used for their capacity to bring insight into what is happening in one's life. Though these intense symbols can be difficult to understand and master, the guidance offered by an experienced practitioner is invaluable when it comes to unlocking the power of runes. Remember that runes should be welcomed as a source of insight rather than something that controls you.

Besides that, shamans can peer into the past, prophesy about the future, and gain insight through stones. Stones are a great way to determine what is on the horizon for yourself. These mystical stones can also be incorporated into rituals of foresight or used as part of your meditative practice.

On the other hand, scrying is an ancient form of divination that requires looking into a reflective surface to uncover patterns, images, or visions. It derives its name from the English word *'descry,'* meaning to catch sight of something with the help of binoculars. When you scry, you can seek answers to questions, search for lost objects and even attempt predictions. This practice is known as *'crystal gazing'* or *'glass gazing.'*

Other forms of shamanic divination include scrying with a reflective surface, throwing runes or bones, and even predicting what is to come. Overall, shamanic divination can give you insight into your life path and spiritual journey and answers about why things are happening in particular ways. With it, you can explore and discover the mysteries of past and future events.

3

Shamanic Healing

Shamanic healing is an ancient practice with transformative power. By engaging in its teachings and rituals, people can connect more deeply with nature, restore harmony across all aspects of their lives and gain insight into their spiritual path. It provides a collaborative, holistic approach to restoring balance and well-being on many levels.

Definition

Shamanic healing has been a part of spiritual and cultural traditions for many centuries, particularly those of indigenous cultures. It is an approach to health care that considers the social, mental, physical, and spiritual aspects of one's well-being, aiming to achieve harmony between them to ensure an optimal state of health. The core belief behind shamanic healing is that illness can result from disruptions in the balance of these components, which must be restored to experience wholeness.

Connecting to the natural world is the foundation of shamanic healing, for it is understood to be the origin of life and well-being. Through rituals, ceremonies, and practices that recognize and celebrate nature's cycles and seasons, this connection can be formed. This relationship allows a shamanic healer to access an ethereal realm to work with spiritual beings such as power animals, leading to healing and equilibrium.

Shamanic healing techniques are diverse and can take many forms, but some of the most common include the following:

- **Power animal retrieval.** Shamanic healers take part in power animal retrieval, which involves traveling to the spirit world to return the spiritual ally and guide of a person who has become disconnected from it. This ancestral tradition is believed to re-establish harmony and well-being in individuals but also carries cultural significance as a reflection of their worldview. Likewise, it is seen as a way to restore balance on an individual level and at a collective level for aboriginal cultures.

- **Soul retrieval.** An age-old practice used by shamanic healers to help restore a person's soul essence, which may have become fragmented or lost due to challenging experiences. Through this spiritual journey, the individual is believed to regain a sense of wholeness and energy. Furthermore, shamans often use meditation and rituals to aid in soul recovery. By doing so, they attempt to balance the person's life and body, allowing them to reconnect with their true selves and move forward with renewed strength.

- **Extraction.** A time-honored practice used for centuries by shamans and spiritual healers to remove negative energies, entities, or thought forms from an individual's body or aura. This process frees the person from low vibrational energies causing physical, mental, or emotional illness or disharmony. Once the extraction is complete, balance and well-being are restored in the person's life.

- **Despacho ceremony.** An ancient and sacred tradition that has been practiced for centuries. It shows appreciation and gratitude for the spirit while helping manifest one's desires and promote healing. Creating a physical offering is integral to the ritual, often in a basket containing food items, flowers, and other sacred objects. Once assembled, the offering is presented to the spirit world with reverence and respect. Additionally, despacho ceremonies are imbued with unique symbolism; each item is carefully included to send specific messages or help clarify intentions or wishes.

- **Sweat lodge ceremony.** Originating from Native American cultures, this ceremony involves entering a small, enclosed structure filled with steam and heat, which is believed to bring renewal, clarity, and healing to a person's physical, emotional, and spiritual aspects. Participants often report feeling revived, rejuvenated, and cleansed after completing the ritual. Likewise, this purifying process enhances healing when a shaman guides the ceremony.

In shamanic healing, the healer collaborates with the person seeking healing. The healer helps guide them through the process, while the person is responsible for their recovery by taking steps towards personal growth and transformation. Shamanic healing is holistic in nature, as it considers all aspects of an individual's physical, emotional, mental, and spiritual when striving to achieve a balanced and healthy state. Additionally, this practice recognizes that true healing necessitates restoring the body and nourishing the mind, heart, and soul. Moreover, it embraces traditional indigenous methods such as rituals, songs, and dancing which can help to facilitate the healing journey.

Aside from that, shamanic healing is a holistic approach to health and wellness that recognizes the power of the mind-body connection. This form of healing goes beyond treating symptoms, offering an in-depth look at the source of any illness. Through its use of rituals, symbols, and traditions, it can help restore balance within the body and heal physical ailments and emotional pain. Lastly, it may assist with positive life transformations, helping people lead healthier and more fulfilling lives.

The Benefits of Shamanic Healing

As such, shamanic healing can provide many physical and spiritual benefits. From alleviating pain to giving spiritual guidance, here is a look at some of the most common advantages associated with shamanic healing:

- **Reconnect with yourself and the world.** One of the primary benefits of shamanic healing is its ability to help individuals reconnect with themselves, their spirits, and the world around them. Through shamanic ceremonies and practices, people can tap into their inner selves and access healing energy. Shamanic healing can also help restore balance in an individual's energy field and provide soul retrieval.

- **Access guidance through power animals.** Power animals are crucial in shamanic healing. These animal spirits can guide an individual in and out of life and provide insight and information about oneself. Shamanic practices such as drumming and meditation help establish a deep connection with one's power animal, offering guidance on navigating life's challenges and gaining new skills for dealing with difficult situations.

- **Discover hidden information.** Shamanic healing practices grant individuals unique access to information ordinarily out of reach. This newfound insight brings greater awareness and understanding, allowing for further personal growth and development. Those who embark on this journey are better equipped to make meaningful changes, leading to an overall improved sense of well-being.

- **Find peace and reconciliation.** Offering a unique way to gain insight and clarity, shamanic practices are often used to guide critical decisions or conflict resolution. Using rituals, drumming, and meditation opens the individual to spiritual realms, allowing them to communicate with their higher self and create inner peace. Shamanic practices also focus on clearing away any negative energy that may block someone from finding peace in their everyday life. This can lead to a deeper understanding and acceptance of oneself and others.

- **Locating lost objects or people.** By entering a trance state, practitioners can access spiritual realms and connect with their higher self or spirit guides to seek guidance on matters such as finding lost objects or people. With heightened awareness, they can often generate leads or clues that reveal the whereabouts of what was thought to be lost. Furthermore, these deep meditative states open the shaman up to the energies of the world around them, providing an intuitive understanding of what might be necessary for successful retrieval.

- **Finding answers and direction:** As an ancient spiritual practice used for centuries, shamanic healing connects individuals to their inner guidance and creates greater clarity and purpose. By using time-honored techniques such as drumming, chanting, divination, meditation, dreamwork, and journeywork, individuals can access deeper levels of consciousness to receive answers and insight into life's questions. Through this practice, individuals can gain insight into their life purpose and direction. With the help of a shamanic guide, practitioners can also find a safe and supportive environment to explore these themes further.

- **Treating various health conditions.** For centuries, shamans have employed varied strategies to heal many physical and mental ailments. Some practices involve herbs and crystals, while others include spiritual dances or chants. This holistic approach often encompasses physical, psychological, and spiritual elements to achieve total health.

- **Safe and natural healing:** Includes various methods such as traditional ritual, meditation, shamanic spirituality, and harnessing the power of nature through plants and stones. Following safety precautions and consulting with an experienced practitioner or healer before beginning your treatment plan is essential when seeking spiritual guidance. Additionally, be aware that shamanic healing is not meant to replace medical care; instead, it can be used with medical interventions for improved quality of life.**Soul retrieval.** Harnessing the power of shamanic healing, soul retrieval is a journey that can help many individuals to restore balance in their energy field. By undertaking this spiritual quest, one can reconnect with themselves and reclaim their spirit and its connection with the world. For those contemplating undergoing soul retrieval, here are some steps to consider:

  ❖ **Find a shaman.** To begin retrieving your soul, looking for a shaman who is an experienced spiritual practitioner is essential. Such a professional can guide you through the procedure, ensuring it is done safely and accurately. Working with an expert in this field guarantees that reconnecting with your innermost essence will be as smooth and enriching as possible. Moreover, shamans also provide valuable advice about how to keep your spirit safe in the future.

  ❖ **Guided meditation exercises.** Allow you to explore parts of yourself that may have been hidden away. As such, your shaman will ask questions about past experiences, including those before and during your birth, to gain insights into the current incarnation. This form of guided self-discovery allows you to clarify areas of your life that you may be struggling with. Likewise, it helps let go of any subconscious blocks or limiting beliefs holding you back from reaching your potential.

❖ **Inward journey.** Embarking on an inward journey with a shaman is essential for self-discovery, unlocking inner potential, and leading to spiritual growth. Various tools such as drumming and singing help uncover underlying issues, beliefs, or values you may have been unaware of. During the journey, the shaman helps you understand and resolve any conflicts or doubts through active reflection, allowing you to find your true purpose in life.

❖ **Reintroduction of missing pieces.** Chanting and meditation can bring back missing parts of yourself that have been suppressed or forgotten and re-integrate them into your being. Doing so can drastically improve physical, emotional, and mental well-being, ultimately leading to finding healing from within. Furthermore, such practices can even help discover hidden aspects of you necessary to create an authentic version of selfhood.

Plant Spirit Medicines

For centuries, shamans have employed the power of plants to heal physical and emotional ailments and restore mental and spiritual balance. In the present day, this practice is still widely applied by shamanic practitioners around the world. Here we look at some of the plants used in plant spirit medicine.

Ayahuasca

Ayahuasca is a potent Amazonian brew made from a combination of an Amazonian vine and the leaves of the Chacruna plant. For thousands of years, indigenous people have utilized this sacred mixture for spiritual healing, medicinal modalities, divination, and spiritual growth. Those who seek it are thought to gain insight and enlightenment from this powerful curative substance, which extends far beyond physical health.

When taken, ayahuasca's dimethyltryptamine (DMT) and MAO inhibitors prevent the breakdown of DMT. Subsequently, it leads to remarkable experiences, including visions, distortions in the perception of reality, and profound spiritual moments. Many who have taken it describe it as awe-inspiring and life-altering. The effects of ayahuasca are unpredictable and can last for several hours, during which time individuals experience vivid and often life-changing visions. Reports include seeing bright colors, intricate geometric patterns, and otherworldly creatures. Others report experiencing a sense of unity with the universe, heightened self-awareness, and profound insights into the nature of reality.

While ayahuasca can be a powerful spiritual tool, it has risks. Negative experiences such as anxiety, paranoia, and panic attacks have been reported. It is also important to note that ayahuasca is illegal in many countries, including the United States. Hence, using it can lead to serious legal consequences. Besides that, traditional ayahuasca ceremonies are highly ritualized and led by a shaman or curandero with extensive knowledge and experience. Without proper guidance and preparation, the use of ayahuasca can be dangerous.

Despite these risks, ayahuasca has gained popularity for spiritual and personal growth. Scientific exploration shows it may also have potential therapeutic advantages in treating depression, addiction, and PTSD. However, as with any powerful substance, ayahuasca should not be taken lightly. Those who choose to consume it must ensure they are in the presence of a knowledgeable and experienced guide aware of its legal implications.

Peyote

The arid expanses of the southwestern United States and northern Mexico are home to the humble and spineless peyote cactus. This plant is steeped in tradition, most notably its usage in Native American religious ceremonies. It is also noteworthy for its psychoactive properties, which are attributed to the alkaloid known as mescaline that it contains. Mescaline has powerful hallucinogenic effects when taken.

For hundreds of years, Native Americans in North America have sought out the psychotropic effects of peyote to take part in spiritual rituals, practice healing, and connect to the divine. Peyote is frequently consumed as a tea or chewed as dried buttons during religious ceremonies, providing participants with various hallucinatory experiences. Used for its psychoactive properties since ancient times, peyote has been an essential part of Native American culture and traditionalism.

Nowadays, peyote has gained popularity as a recreational drug, and its use has become more widespread. When consumed, mescaline produces a range of psychoactive effects, including hallucinations, changes in perception, and altered states of consciousness. The results of mescaline can be intense and last for several hours, and the experience is often described as both profound and mystical.

Despite its popularity and longstanding history, peyote carries risks that should not be overlooked. Mescaline has been known to cause many unpleasant side effects, such as nausea, vomiting, and rapid heartbeat. Moreover, the effects of consuming it can be unpredictable, leading to feelings of anxiety, paranoia, and panic in some cases. Furthermore, there is the potential for accidental poisoning due to confusion in identifying the plant correctly *(Faria, 2021)*. Lastly, even with its designation as a controlled substance, peyote is still widely used, often sold illicitly.

Overall, rich in culture and powerful in effects, peyote is a cactus containing the psychoactive compound mescaline. While its use boasts a long history among Native American cultures, it has gained popularity as a recreational drug. Those considering peyote must be aware of potential side effects and approach it with caution.

Datura

Datura is a plant that has gained notoriety for its poisonous and hallucinogenic properties. It is part of the Solanaceae family, which includes vegetables like tomatoes, peppers, and potatoes. This type of plant is native to dry climates worldwide, with habitats including desert areas in North America and Central Asia, plus certain tropical regions. Although it can be dangerous if misused, it has a long history as a medicinal aid and ceremonial accompaniment.

With its large, fragrant white or purple trumpet-shaped flowers and spiky green leaves, datura is a plant that has been used for centuries in both medicinal and spiritual practices. In traditional Native American cultures, it served as a painkiller and an avenue to connect with the spiritual realm. Other societies also used datura as an interrogation tool, using the plant as a truth serum to extract confessions from criminal suspects. Lastly, ayurvedic medicine is employed in India to cure various ailments, such as digestive and respiratory illnesses.

However, using datura carries significant risks, as the plant is highly poisonous. Dangerous levels of tropane alkaloids, which can result in delirium, delirium tremens, and unconsciousness, are present in every part of the plant. Overdose of datura can lead to death, and even in small amounts, the plant can cause serious health problems, including irregular heartbeat, high blood pressure, and respiratory failure.

Despite these risks, datura has been used for recreational purposes for its hallucinogenic effects. The plant's alkaloids produce intense and vivid hallucinations, and users report feelings of detachment, euphoria, and a distorted sense of time. Some people also report experiencing terrifying and traumatic hallucinations, which can lead to long-term psychological harm.

In addition to its toxic effects, datura is highly invasive, and its spread can be difficult to control. The plant can quickly take over an ecosystem, out-competing native species and disrupting the local flora and fauna balance. This can significantly impact the environment, making it a danger to human health and the natural world. Yet, despite its dangers, datura continues to be used for its medicinal and spiritual properties. In modern times, its use has been regulated and is only allowed under certain conditions and with proper supervision. For example, some countries allow its use for spiritual purposes in religious ceremonies, but only if the plant is used in a controlled and supervised environment.

Altogether, datura, a plant that thrives in desert climates, is renowned for its potentially fatal and mind-altering effects. For centuries, it has been used for medicinal and spiritual purposes; however, these applications come with serious risks. Death, debilitating health issues, and environmental damage are just some consequences of misusing this plant. To stay safe, always heed the advice of an experienced datura practitioner before using it in any setting.

Psilocybin Mushrooms

Psilocybin mushrooms, a type of fungus containing the psychedelic drug psilocybin, have long been revered by indigenous people across the globe for their spiritual and medicinal properties. These mushrooms are known to cause hallucinations and other effects on the human mind that have piqued curiosity among researchers and enthusiasts alike. Recently, there has been an increasing fascination with the therapeutic potential of psilocybin, leading to a renewed interest in studying the effects of these mushrooms on the human mind.

Mushrooms are a source of psilocybin, including varieties like:

- *Psilocybe cubensis* (gold top)
- *Psilocybe mexicana* (mexican)
- *Panaeolus subbalteatus* (panaeolus)

Salvia Divinorum

Salvia divinorum, commonly called *"Sage of the Diviners,"* is a psychoactive plant hailing from the Oaxaca region of Mexico. Salvinorin A's primary constituent is a potent and highly selective kappa opioid receptor agonist. This means that it uniquely affects certain brain receptors compared to what is seen with other common psychoactive substances such as LSD, marijuana, and ecstasy. The experience these effects bring forth are dramatic alterations in one's perspective, thought process, and emotions that all last for 15 to 30 minutes.

Salvinorin A's precise processes of operation have yet to be completely comprehended. Nonetheless, it is thought to alter how data is processed in the brain. Reports from some individuals describe extreme visual and auditory hallucinations, while others speak of disconnection from reality and enhanced self-reflection. The effects of salvia divinorum often elicit a feeling of traveling to other realms or having intense, dream-like experiences. This has piqued the interest of many individuals and generated curiosity about its potential for healing those suffering from depression, anxiety, and post-traumatic stress disorder. While these effects can be highly unusual, they provide an intriguing opportunity to explore alternative therapies for complex mental health issues.

Despite its potential benefits, the use of salvia divinorum carries some risks. Its potency can lead to adverse effects, including intense anxiety, paranoia, and hallucinations. Furthermore, little is known about the consequences of prolonged use of this substance on the body and mind. As such, more research must be conducted to assess its potential dangers.

Over the past few years, salvia divinorum has become increasingly popular, primarily amongst young people. This rise in usage has sparked debates regarding its potential for abuse and possible consequences. While some countries and states have prohibited selling and possessing salvia divinorum, others have limited its availability with restrictions. This psychoactive plant has been used medically and to reach spiritual heights for centuries. Its active ingredient, salvinorin A, offers a unique experience that is highly personal and can differ greatly between individuals. Although research is still required to comprehend any associated risks fully, this plant's therapeutic potential is clear. Thus, it is essential to pay attention to its use today and educate the public about its possible effects.

Kava Kava

For centuries, kava has been renowned for its soothing and anxiolytic properties. Native to the South Pacific islands, it is a species of pepper widely grown in Fiji, Tonga, and Vanuatu. Its root is used to make kava, an ancient beverage cherished for its tranquilizing effects by many indigenous cultures. Sipping on this libation is thought to improve mental well-being and create a feeling of serenity, perfect for unwinding after a long day.

Making kava starts with grounding the plant's roots to create a thick, muddy liquid. With its distinct and slightly bitter taste, this beverage is often enjoyed in social settings for celebrations or as an effective relaxing method after a long day. But the properties that make it unique come from kavalactones, the active ingredients in kava that provide sedative and anxiolytic effects. Not only can kava leave you feeling calmer, more content, and positively minded, but research has also suggested its mild pain-relieving qualities, proving helpful in treating insomnia, anxiety, and even menstrual cramps.

Research has uncovered the potential of kava to treat mental health conditions such as depression and anxiety. In some cases, the results show that it can be as effective as medication without unwanted side effects. Moreover, kava has a low risk of addiction and abuse, making it an attractive alternative for those seeking a natural remedy for mental health issues.

Besides that, the traditional drink kava has been consumed in the South Pacific islands for centuries, having been known to provide potential benefits to those suffering from anxiety and depression. However, its use should be done carefully as there are possible side effects and risks that can come with consuming large amounts of the beverage. Reports have even linked the long-term use of kava with liver toxicity and, in extreme cases, failure. Therefore, before consuming any kava, it is crucial to talk to a healthcare professional and become aware of the associated risks and possible interactions with other medications.

Medicine Wheel and Four Directions

The medicine wheel, known as the four directions, is a long-established tool for shamanism and healing. It represents balance, growth, and harmony used by indigenous people across the world for thousands of years. These four directions symbolize the physical aspects of the cosmos, along with their spiritual forces. North is associated with air; east with fire; south with water; and west with earth. Furthermore, each direction is linked to particular plants, animals, and colors, offering additional ways to access its power. By connecting with this powerful source wisely, we can discover our full spiritual potential.

Shamans can use the medicine wheel as a tool to aid in decision-making. It helps us find the answers to questions about our lives, such as:

- What should I do for work?
- Am I ready for a relationship?
- Where do I want to live?

Likewise, to explore your options thoroughly, try asking questions from different directions to see which is with you. For instance, you could question, *"What is my next step?"* and listen for responses from various directions. Pay attention to your body's sensations as you listen for answers. As such, if you hear *"apprentice with me"* from one direction and it feels right, follow that path. However, do not pursue it if it does not sit well with you for any reason, such as poor timing or other factors.

Yet, if you do not have a particular action path, trust your intuition. Listen closely to the signs you encounter and more on how this works later. Another thing you can do is evaluate what would make you happiest right now and consider how you would like your life or yourself to look differently than they currently do. The medicine wheel is an excellent tool for aiding decision-making and can also be very helpful in bouncing back from bad choices and making better decisions overall.

Examining the medicine wheel will make you aware of the energy in each direction; *north, south, east, and west.* This ancient tool can unlock hidden patterns previously not apparent or noticeable. It will help you recognize how the physical, mental, and spiritual parts intertwine in ways you may not have noticed before. When you see your life from a new perspective, you will begin to identify connections between events and relationships that have gone unnoticed.

Use this tool to make decisions daily. As you come to any choice, such as what to have for dinner or which work project you want to take up next week, reflect and ask yourself which direction best aligns with your values and life purpose. If a particular direction resonates strongly with you, pursue it. Moreover, this tool can be applied when making important decisions, such as where to live or whom to marry. As such, when joining into long-term commitments like marriage or having children, consider your dreams and goals alongside those of the people you are venturing forth with. Through rituals like medicine wheel ceremonies, you can envision the future and make informed choices about your life that could lead you closer to your desired outcomes.

Moreover, decision-making can be shaped by the four directions tool and the medicine wheel, which serve as a shamanic guide for navigating life. This tool can be highly beneficial for making decisions in life, as it helps understand different viewpoints within an issue and to anticipate the consequences before acting upon them. For instance, the eagle represents the east, representing vision and energy. When you establish a clear picture of your life, you transmit power to make it happen. Therefore, if you think negatively, that thought becomes more assertive and can become your reality; similarly, if you think positively, likewise will be what comes out of it.

Pillar 2
Spirits

Unlocking the secrets of pillar two of shamanism is an exciting journey that dives into the concept of spirits. From finding your spirit guides and angels to exploring the primordial deity and water entities, you can gain valuable insight into building a solid connection with the spiritual realm. Discovering how to communicate with spirit guides while learning the importance of water spirits helps you better understand this practice and its role in our lives.

4

Spirit Guides

Have you ever wondered how your spirit guides appear? They may appear to you as benevolent guardian angels or powerful animals such as wolves or bears. But even if these spiritual allies have never crossed your mind, you must remain aware of their presence and prioritize constantly hearing and connecting with them.

Connecting with Your Spirit Guides

Pay close attention to your intuition. Embrace it. Stay open to God's voice and the presence of those who have passed away in your lives, who love unconditionally and yearn for your contentment and well-being. Sometimes, you experience signs from your spirit guides that are subtly hinted, such as a bird crashing into the window or a song played on the radio at an opportune moment. Synchronicity also plays its part when two unrelated events occur together so that it feels like they were designed to be fused. For example, if you find yourself pondering about someone, then suddenly receive an email from them or unexpectedly come across them in person, it could signify that the other person is picking up on your thoughts. Have you been noticing these signs of unexplained occurrences in your day-to-day life? Perhaps, one of your spirit guides is trying to communicate with you. To make it easier for them, meditation can be a perfect way to create an open communication channel. By calming your mind and focusing on the here and now, you can let go of any negative thoughts or emotions that might interfere. This allows you to connect with your spirit guide and receive their messages.

As such, do the following steps to meditate effectively.

- **Step 1:** Designate a time for yourself, away from distractions like the ever-present social media. Find a period where you are awake and alert, not too tired or sleepy.
- **Step 2:** Ensure total comfort by sitting on the floor or in a chair with your feet flat. Consider folding one leg under yourself if necessary, but be sure to distribute pressure throughout your body evenly.
- **Step 3:** Make sure the position is natural and comfortable, using pillows to support your knees if sitting cross-legged is uncomfortable for you. However, keep those pillows from rising too high, as they can disrupt circulation into and out of certain areas.
- **Step 4:** Close your eyes as this process begins so you will focus inwardly on your breath or a specific mantra that resonates with you.

Connecting with your spiritual self yields a myriad of rewards. Psychic healing is an energy-based process centered around the power of intuition. Through this form of healing, you can explore your journey of self-discovery, forge a connection with your guardian angels, and uncover your life's divine mission. With the expertise of a spiritual guide, you can also utilize their divine knowledge to assist in completing any tasks or challenges you face.

For instance, if you desired to create a book with the aid of a spiritual mentor, you could utter the following words: *"I would appreciate the wisdom of my angelic guardian or any divine force present in this space right now."* Then, calmly wait for their counsel to enter your head or maybe even be written down.

Subsequently, reach out to your spirit guides and ask them for their names. By doing so, you can establish a connection with them. You could also invite them to appear in some form so that you can see and hear what they have to say; this could be through vivid dreams or drawings created by children. Request for messages which will guide your life at this moment. Furthermore, it is recommended that you take time each day to meditate and seek insights from these spiritual entities if something feels off in your physical or mental state. Be open to receiving their revelations verbally or even through writing. Moreover, certain spiritual practices like crystal healing may aid in connecting with your guides and heighten the clarity of their messages.

Your Higher Self

At first, I used to feel lost and unsure of who I was. It took me a while to come to terms with this feeling and realize that feeling disconnected from oneself or the world around us is typical. As such, trying to make sense of something without understanding the language or context can be tricky, like reading a book written in a foreign language. Without knowing the words, grammar rules, and meaning behind our reading, how can it have any real impact? Knowledge is often the key to unlocking a deeper understanding and appreciation for our lives and those around us. With this in mind, our identity is no wonder essential in defining who we are and why it matters.

Connecting to your higher self can provide clarity when making decisions and guidance on moving forward. By trusting and following your intuition, you are investing in yourself and engaging with something more significant than what can be seen in the physical world. Additionally, through meditation and stillness, you can connect more deeply to your higher self by allowing the mind to become calm and open. This opens the communication channels between you and your higher self, giving you access to wisdom from within.

Aside from that, your heart can be your best guide. It may help you make sense of an emotional and challenging situation or prepare for what is to come. Facial expressions or body language can reveal their feelings and intentions without words. Pay attention to physical sensations as well; a hint of pain, tightness, or anything else that does not feel right can alert you to the presence of danger or tell you something important needs addressing. Often, prompt action is essential to ensure nothing worse happens. To sum up, tuning into your intuition and body responses can provide invaluable insights and lead you in the right direction.

Likewise, *have you ever wondered what connecting with your higher self is like?* Drawing on your inner wisdom and tapping into it through meditation or journaling can help you gain clarity, understanding, and purpose. Your higher self knows all about you, like your strengths and weaknesses, and what brings you joy. Moreover, it is a source of unconditional love, compassion, and guidance. When asking questions like *"What do I need to know?"*, *"How can I best serve others?"* be still and open to receiving answers in the form of thoughts or feelings in your mind or body. It can be as simple as *"I should take more time for myself"* or *"I feel frustrated when people do not listen."* This connection will provide insight into how to live an authentic life in alignment with your truth.

When hearing your inner wisdom, you need to listen closely and without judgment. Meditation and journaling are great ways to open communication channels between you and your internal guidance. One helpful step is getting in touch with your heart, letting it speak freely by tuning out the noise and focusing on your feelings. Taking even a few moments each day for self-reflection or spending time in nature can help you better understand yourself and your intuition.

Furthermore, finding inner peace and connecting with your spiritual self can be done through meditation or journaling. Meditation can be practiced as early as the first morning hour or as late as before you drift off to sleep. To find what works best for you, play around with open and closed eyes, silence, or music. Additionally, documenting your thoughts and feelings in a journal allows you to gain clarity on now and past experiences while providing an avenue to express gratitude for all the good things in life.

Meanwhile, as you take the time to pause and listen to the whisper of your inner guidance, you can gain access to an unlimited source of knowledge. This inner wisdom speaks the truth, informing you about yourself and others. When a negative thought or emotion arises in reaction to something that has occurred, it often reflects a truth within you, even if ego obscures part of the picture. For example, getting angry at someone for criticizing your physical appearance could be a sign that their words resonated with you on some level. Though such comments may have been directed with malicious intent, there is likely still an element of truth present. Embracing this new-found insight can help you develop further understanding and appreciation for yourself and others.

In general, you can access your higher self through various activities, such as meditation, prayer, journaling, and creative expression. A pivotal step to connecting with this aspect of yourself is to foster an inner dialogue and accept whatever feelings or messages come your way. Your higher self illuminates the path forward on your journey toward personal growth, joy, and transformation. By tuning into its wisdom, you can overcome fear and build resilience in life's challenges. All you need is an open heart, trust in the process, and faith that you will be led in the right direction.

Angels and Archangels

Angels are spiritual messengers that can bring relief, peace, and strength. Many cultures honor the presence of angels, including Christianity and Judaism. Members of these religions believe that certain archangels have been appointed to watch over specific areas such as health, livelihoods, and protection. Moreover, many believe angels can intercede on our behalf during struggle or hardship. With the right intentions and an open heart, connecting with the angelic realm is easier than you may think. It is often a matter of simply speaking your request aloud or asking for help in times of distress.

Understanding the distinction between angels and archangels is essential. Although both beings fall under the 'angel' heading, it is crucial to recognize that they are not interchangeable. While angels are typically described as messengers from God, archangels serve more specific missions, such as protecting individuals or providing guidance for human events. Furthermore, some religious texts designate seven archangels: *Michael, Raphael, Gabriel, Uriel, Sariel, Raguel, and Remiel.*

Thus, angels and archangels are celestial beings who serve God differently. Angels act as messengers between humans and God, while archangels have more power and are high-ranking members of heaven's army. As such, they carry out God's will on Earth and interact with humans directly to provide guidance or protection in times of crisis or despair. For instance, the archangel Michael is known to appear before people to keep them safe during dangerous situations like war zones. These divine protectors also have strong ties with humanity; providing invaluable counsel and support when needed can make a difference for individuals experiencing difficulties. This highlights how angels and archangels differ: the former are guides that help us through our daily lives, while the latter holds immense authority from heavenly realms.

Have you ever experienced the presence of an angel? Many believe that angels exist around us and can manifest in different ways. For some, it may be a dream, vision, or even a faint scent of something sweet. Others may see symbols such as birds or butterflies, which could indicate an angel is nearby. Everywhere we turn, angels may attempt to reach us, yet we may not be aware of them. To know if a messenger from above is trying to communicate, look out for strange behavior from animals or brief glimpses of light. Even if something appears normal at first glance, it could be a sign that something meaningful is happening nearby. It is also worth noting that angels are believed to arise as signs of love and protection, making paying attention to their subtle signals even more important.

Altogether, angels and archangels are powerful spiritual beings that can intervene in matters related to human life. Invoking the aid of these divine agents can provide guidance, comfort, and hope when we need it most. They are here to help if we remain open-minded, mindful, and prayerful. If we earnestly desire a deeper understanding of our place in the world or seek answers to our prayers and inquiries, they will be there with unconditional love and support. Additionally, angels are often seen as mysterious creatures responsible for miraculous events like protecting a lost child or healing from an illness that seemed incurable. These occurrences, however, often go unnoticed or even dismissed by those without faith in their power. Belief in an unseen force helping guide us is critical to understanding their presence and strength.

Ancestors

Feeling a connection to the past is something many of us can relate to. That sense of legacy and responsibility can be extreme for those with a long family history steeped in stories and traditions. *But what if you could access more than just your family tree?* Ancestors, after all, can serve as spirit guides, healing from painful experiences, resolving past issues, and offering emotional support during times of turmoil. Though asking them for help with everyday problems like chores may feel strange or intimidating initially, understanding why calling on ancestors' wisdom makes sense and how simple it is to make contact is critical. As such, it is worth considering what they might answer when you ask for their advice and the historical knowledge they could share that could benefit you in finding solutions.

Not only can ancestors help us with the everyday problems that arise in life, but they often have deeper wisdom and insight from being beyond this physical plane. They can offer counsel on issues that are far more difficult to answer or are emotional and give guidance on long-term goals or larger visions for our lives. Here we can also uncover why taking up contact with ancestors is not so strange after all. In fact, it is a form of honoring those who came before us, and turning to their experience and knowledge has been done throughout many cultures for centuries. By engaging with our ancestral guides, we may find answers, learn lessons, open ourselves up to our intuition, and live much closer to our ancestors' vision.

Understanding your ancestors' past can give you an even broader perspective on life. Looking towards the traditions and beliefs of our ancestors is also a great way to uncover the secrets of meaningful living. With access to their wisdom, you could gain insights into how they approached challenges and navigated difficult situations to make wise decisions. Additionally, honoring the memory of your ancestors can be rewarding and empowering at times when you feel lost or overwhelmed. By connecting with those who have gone before us, we can learn from their experiences and use them as a source of strength for tackling whatever life might throw.

You can ask your ancestors for help with the following:

- Discover your spiritual path and establish a connection with the divine.
- Foster meaningful relationships with people, including family members and partners.
- Prioritize physical and mental health for total well-being.
- Create financial abundance for yourself and your loved ones, pursue success in career or business ventures, and maintain strong family dynamics.

Remember, our ancestors are not just from a different place but from within us. They can offer guidance, support, and consolation; all we need to do is call upon them. To make a strong connection with an ancestor, it can be helpful to practice meditation or other relaxation techniques to become more open to the messages of your ancestor. Additionally, knowledge of your ancestors' culture, customs, and indigenous language may help create a stronger link between you and them.

However, staying in touch with our ancestors can be challenging. To help overcome this difficulty, consider asking yourself questions such as:

- How does this person view me?
- What advice would they give me about my current plans?
- What do I need from them right now?

Asking these types of questions can help us connect with our ancestors. As such, by considering how an ancestor might view us or what advice they would give, we can understand our family history and culture and how it may be relevant to our current situation.

When trying to find answers to these questions, it helps to reach within for answers that come from your own experience and knowledge. Writing down what comes up can be a powerful way to gain insight into situations and uncover solutions. Lastly, it is also wise to seek advice from others who have gone through similar experiences or may even have passed away; they may offer advice to help you navigate the challenge.

Plants

Have you ever considered having a plant as a spiritual guide? Plants can be more than just decoration; they offer an invaluable source of comfort and support, no matter what happens in your life. Even when facing the toughest questions, plants can provide healing and balance for your emotions. Plus, their calming presence can help ground you and bring clarity to your energy.

Since ancient times, plants have been revered for their healing and spiritual powers. Links between plants and spiritual practices like shamanism, centered around the belief that everything has a soul and is connected, can be traced back 30,000 years. Shamans use medicinal plants to treat physical and emotional ailments like depression and anxiety. They believe that connecting with the energy of plants through rituals can help them tap into their spirit guides, ancestors, guardian angels, animal spirit guides, and other forms of protection. Not only is this a potent form of healing. Yet, it can also bring clarity that helps guide us through life's struggles.

Connecting to your plant spirit guide is like connecting with any other spiritual mentor and goes beyond simply conversing. To create an effective connection, you must be open and receptive to the plant's energies while willing to take time from your day. Additionally, understanding the symbolic meaning of plants can help establish a strong bond with them. Embracing a ritualistic approach, such as connecting under the guidance of rituals or meditations, can further deepen the connection between you and your plant spirit guide.

In establishing a meaningful connection with your plant spirit guide, ask them vocally or mentally if they want to join you on your journey. Alternatively, visit their environment and observe them in their natural habitat. If neither of these options is appealing, take some time to think about what qualities an ideal companion should possess that could be beneficial in helping you progress in your growth and development or aiding you in the challenges presented by our lives on this planet. Additionally, remember that plants are living entities: *connecting with them starts with treating them with respect and kindness.* Showing care for the world around us is one way of developing strong relationships with other life forms.

Hence, plants are incredible living beings that have existed since the dawn. They have a deep connection to the earth, and many believe that plants possess a spirit and can be helpful to human guides. To begin working with plant spirit guides, it is essential to identify which one will work best for you. You may already have an affinity for a specific type of plant, or you could explore your neighborhood and observe different types of trees or wildflowers in local parks or gardens. Once you have identified a specific plant, the next step is to get familiar with its unique characteristics and behavior. This will help deepen your connection and allow you access to insights and wisdom only this plant can provide.

Animals

Throughout all cultures, spirit animals have been used to connect the spiritual and physical realms. With their guidance, people can better understand who they are and their place in the world. As such, through rituals and activities, one can connect with their spirit animal to discover valuable insights about life. This part of the book will guide you in exploring this spiritual journey and unlocking the power within yourself that their spirit animal symbolizes.

People have long believed that animals are more than just physical entities and have unique abilities to reveal spiritual truths. For example, in many Native American tribes, totems or talismans are used to invoke the spirit of an animal and its traits. These can be seen to honor and pay tribute to the wisdom of these animals. With the help of these animal spirit guides, people can gain insight into their spiritual journey and personal growth. Additionally, shamans utilize not only herbs and various plants for healing but animal medicines as well. Animal medicines can come in various forms, such as extracts, parts (like fur or bones), or the whole animal.

Thinking of spirit animals often recalls Native American totems, potent symbols reflecting an animal's spirit and personality. These totems vary in interpretation among tribes. For instance, some believe that only certain animals have essences that can be used as totems. Meanwhile, others believe that all living creatures have spirits, explaining the use of various animals as symbols for human qualities such as strength or bravery. Regardless of interpretation, spirit animals can teach us about ourselves and help us connect with the natural world around us. For example, suppose your totem animal is the coyote. In that case, you adapt quickly, much like how coyotes are known for adapting to changing circumstances in their environment.

Perhaps, you may have noticed that certain animals draw you in, prompting you to ponder what deeper meanings they could be representing. Psychologists believe humans can utilize their hearts and instincts when making decisions, otherwise known as a "gut feeling," rather than relying solely on logic. A few prominent examples of animals and their related symbolism are owls which signify wisdom. Then, wolves stand for strength and leadership, while snakes represent transformation. If an animal's characteristics mirror yours, it could symbolize something about your life path or serve as a spiritual guide. To further understand the connection between yourself and animals, seek expert advice on animal symbolism and use their findings to help make better-informed decisions.

The presence of a spirit animal in your life indicates that you are connected to the spiritual realm in some way. It can symbolize strength in difficult times or guide you during personal journeys of self-exploration. Commonly, a spirit animal is associated with a particular emotion or state of being. Others believe they provide protection and wisdom to those who need it most. Additionally, it is said that each person may have more than one spirit animal associated with them at any given time. Seeing what kind of animals appear in your daily life, whether through dream sequences, artworks, or unexpected occurrences, can help you recognize the spiritual signs connecting you to all living creatures.

Linking with your animal totem can be done by looking at what it stands for in the astrological system. Astrology is a tool that allows us to gain deeper insight into ourselves and our lives based on the stars and planets. To learn more about this subject, explore the many books available on Amazon or at your local bookstore. Some people also turn to online sources such as blogs, podcasts, and webinars to access astrological information.

Deities

Developing a shamanic belief system means familiarizing yourself with its different associated deities. While there is a vast array of gods and goddesses, some are more prominent than others, such as Odin, Ra, Amaterasu, and Quetzalcoatl. Furthermore, each deity carries its powers and responsibilities, often reflecting the beliefs and values of the given culture or region. Understanding all its associated gods is essential to truly understand the construct of a shamanic belief system.

The Primordial Deity

The primordial deity is the origin of all existence. As such, its power allows for manifestation and control over all physical and metaphysical realities. This includes providing life and guidance to mortals, manipulating time and space, and creating other dimensions outside our reality. Many cultures honor this being as a divine and omnipotent figure due to their boundless capabilities, which have always been present even before recorded time. Along with this immense power comes the responsibility of maintaining balance in the universe by controlling both good and evil forces. These abilities are attributed to the primordial deity, integral to many historical and spiritual beliefs.

The Sky Deity

Across nearly every religion and culture, sky gods have been revered for their power over the elements. Moreover, the sky deity is often envisioned as an older man with long white hair perched atop a rainbow and eyes closed. This symbolizes his protective watch over the world without any interference, except when necessary. He may also be portrayed donning wings akin to those of an angel or wearing a headdress adorned with feathers like those worn by Native Americans in the battle against other tribes or nations in colonial days. In many cultures, this figure is associated with wisdom and guidance; he offers advice and protection despite not being involved directly. His knowledge is said to be vast and superior to mere mortals.

The ancient Greeks called their sky god *Zeus*, while other cultures used names like *Toran, Thor, Tāwhirimātea,* and *Indra.* In most stories involving a sky god, they are believed to be capable of controlling the weather by manipulating winds and rain. Additionally, they are usually seen as responsible for protecting people from natural disasters such as floods and storms by using mighty thunderbolts or lightning bolts. Ultimately, these gods were believed to oversee the sun's and stars' day-to-day movements across the sky.

The Sky Deity's Family

The sky god is the head of the pantheon and has a family, including:

- **Sun.** Providing light and warmth to sustain life.
- **Moon.** Illuminating the darkness, working alongside the stars as they shine brightly at night.

- **Stars.** Seen as the progeny of the sun, illuminating the night sky with their persistent glimmer.

In addition to these three major deities, many others represent different aspects of nature: wind, rain, and earth are part of this pantheon's family tree.

The Earth Mother

The Earth's mother is the world's creator and is responsible for every inhabitant. Revered as a goddess of agriculture and fertility, her rule spans plants, animals, forests, and waters. She provides her people with their daily needs so they can exist in harmony with each other and nature while leading content lives. As an expression of deep respect towards her impact on life and fertility, many cultures have celebrated the Earth mother through seasonal feasts such as Lammas or Imbolc.

The Water Spirits

Legends abound of water spirits worldwide, from kappa in Japan to nāga in India. Water spirits are seen as powerful and mysterious entities that inhabit rivers, lakes, and other bodies of water. Their demeanor towards human beings can vary depending on their type. Some are mischievous or evil, while others may be kind and benevolent.

The Ancestors

Our ancestors are an integral part of the spiritual belief system for shamans. They have passed down their wisdom and teachings through shared stories, tales, and legends over generations. Shamanism teaches that these ancestors remain close to us in human form, guiding us through life. Additionally, it is believed that the spirits of one's family, tribe, and people linger within them, granting insight into the ancestral roots that define who they are.

Altogether, ancient shamanic beliefs are based on honoring and connecting with the gods and goddesses who control the elements and influence human lives. To do this, followers of those belief systems pray to their chosen deities regularly and engage in rituals that have symbolic meanings. Knowing about these deities helps us gain insight into how the world works, and it can be a source of understanding for life's events. Additionally, to experience favorable growth, we must recognize, acknowledge, and thank those deities for their help. Honoring them gives us access to our hidden knowledge, intuition, and power.

Pillar 3
Journey

The third pillar of shamanism, the journey, is where the real work starts. We will uncover the various paths to achieving a shamanic state of consciousness, including soul flight, meditation, and rituals. Doing so gives us access to spirit guides, ancestors, and other entities in the shamanic world, which can provide unique insights and understanding of our lives and the world around us. Here we delve into the different techniques and tools shamans use to embark on their journeys and how you can use them to enhance your spiritual practice while connecting you with those unseen realms.

5

What Is a Shamanic Journey

Shamanic journeys are a type of deep meditation that offers the opportunity to explore the depths of your inner self and gain insight into yourself and situations you face. Through guided visualization, you can access your intuition and gain clarity on matters.

Soul Flight

Taking to the skies can be thrilling if it is your dream. Shamanic soul flight is an ancient practice where you leave your physical body to explore different realms. It may be done through meditation, a shamanic journey or ceremony, or even with the help of certain drugs. Through soul flight, we can gain communication with spirit helpers and discover new locations and insights. Mastering this skill requires practice, and it is best to have assistance from an experienced shaman to guide the first few flights for safety and security.

As such, embarking on the journey of soul flight requires some preparation. To gain control over the experience and to ensure a successful takeoff, one must acquire good grounding skills and be in touch with their body and mind. An excellent place to start is to find a peaceful location, perhaps without much interference, and sit comfortably in front of an altar or table with personal significance. Taking three deep breaths allows one to set their intentions for the journey ahead and focus on their inner visualizations. From here, imagine yourself soaring high above your home or neighborhood, witnessing all that lies below from a divine perspective.

Acquiring knowledge about soul flight is essential. However, that is not enough. Regular practice is necessary to experience the sensations of leaving your body. Find a trusted teacher to guide you on this journey and commit to sticking with the sessions. Even experienced shamans find it difficult during their earlier flights. So, do not be disheartened if progress is not instantaneous; take your time, practice diligently, and fly safely.

Practicing Shamanic Journeying

Shamanic journeying is an ancient practice rooted in the wisdom of indigenous cultures that enables individuals to attain knowledge and strength to heal the planet and its inhabitants. This journey is a way to gain insight into one's true self, discover authority, and access other worlds. It provides an opportunity to find accurate understanding, healing, and transformation. The shamanic journey is a path of recovery, awareness, and empowerment; it is a way to unlock the power necessary for revitalizing the earth and its people.

Going on a shamanic journey is a profound and enlightening experience. It can involve various activities such as drumming and trance dancing to enter an altered state, chanting prayers or mantras, or engaging in mindful meditation. All of these offer the individual an opportunity to receive information about their inner self and uncover hidden aspects of their life and identity. This newfound knowledge can be used for personal advancement and shared with others, creating positive change in the world. Thus, shamanic journeying is a path to empowerment and a powerful tool for awakening our true potential.

Over the years, I have been practicing shamanism, and it can be explored in many ways. It can be used as a healing tool or an initiation process to reach higher levels of power within oneself or those who accompanied you on your journey. Besides these, it can also be used as a chance to dive deeper into yourself without any predetermined goal other than gaining more knowledge through self-reflection and insight while immersed in *"the world"* beyond our physical reality.

Shamans use shamanic journeying to connect with spiritual realms, allowing them to interact with spirits and deities and heal themselves by entering an altered state of consciousness. Yet, it does not stop at shamans; anyone can learn how to do it. For thousands of years, this practice has been used by indigenous people worldwide to create bonds between their world and what they call *'the divine.'* Even today, shamans in different ceremonies across the globe are practicing shamanic journeying.

To begin your ceremony, set up a sacred space. Light candles or incense to create a ritualistic atmosphere. Place the drum on an altar or table so it is visible to all participants. Invoke each directional guardian one by one: *east (air), south (fire), west (water), and north (earth)*. Feel their unique energy as they enter from all four directions around you; visualize their presence filling the circle. Ask if any other helping spirits would like to join and if anyone needs healing work done on them at this time. Then with full awareness, embark on your spiritual journey together.

Gaining Insights Through Meditation and Rituals

Meditation is a form of training for the mind and body and is an excellent way to become more conscious of your thoughts and feelings. Incense has been an integral part of religious ceremonies for centuries, having a calming effect on both the practitioner and the environment. Not only does it create a relaxing atmosphere, but it also helps to clear away lingering negative energy while allowing positive vibrations to arise. Combining incense with meditation can be helpful to deepen concentration and focus, allowing one to benefit from its meditative effects in shorter time frames. Additionally, using incense during meditation also has spiritual and physical health benefits, such as reducing stress levels, promoting mental clarity, and relieving anxiety.

Subsequently, meditation has long been linked with improved physical and mental health, cognitive functioning, creativity, and productivity. By observing our internal state of being and listening to our thoughts, we can gain insight into ourselves and better handle life's challenges.

Likewise, practice meditation with a guide or instructor; guided meditation. With guided meditation, the power to unlock your potential lies within your mind. A skilled instructor or guide can provide you with the knowledge and guidance needed to get the most out of your practice. Numerous studies have shown that spending even a short amount of time meditating daily can significantly improve your physical, mental, and emotional health. Additionally, research suggests that guided meditation can help reduce cortisol levels in the body, thus promoting relaxation and well-being.

Rituals are also a powerful tool for self-discovery. In fact, many spiritual traditions rely on rituals to deepen their connection to something greater than themselves. Through rituals, we can encounter new perspectives or gain insight and clarity on a situation or thought process previously elusive and challenging to grasp. Additionally, they can be used as an opportunity for personal transformation by actively engaging in activities that help us explore who we are and what lies beyond our comfort zones. These practices allow us to reflect on the present moment so that we may move forward from it with greater meaning and purpose.

On the other hand, mantras are a form of meditation that can help you gain insights and clarity. Not only are they associated with religious practices, but they can also represent personal affirmations. For instance, you might constantly repeat *"I am grateful"* to remind you of gratitude. Or perhaps, you may use the mantra *"I am going after my dream job"* as a reminder of your goals. Apart from being used as affirmations and reminders, mantras can also be used to focus during yoga or mindfulness practice, allowing for deep relaxation and improved psychological health.

Hence, to unwind and practice meditation, use incense. As mentioned, incense has long been used to promote relaxation and meditation. Burning them can have numerous benefits, from calming the mind and reducing stress to increased focus. It can be used in various ways, from energizing yoga practice to helping to create an atmosphere for prayer or reflection. In fact, ancient mystics believed incense could transport prayers directly to the divine realm, or gods, for answers and guidance.

Additionally, different types of incense have their associations with different meanings; for instance, sandalwood relates to peace and tranquility, while jasmine is associated with spiritual awakening. As such, incense can also include healing properties depending on the chosen type, creating a unique ambiance. Furthermore, many kinds of incense contain natural essential oils, providing additional aromatherapeutic benefits. With so many diverse options available, there is sure to be an incense that appeals to everyone's preferences and needs.

Embodying the Practice

Staying connected to our spiritual path is essential for maintaining a sense of well-being. This book offers practical advice to help readers incorporate spirituality into their daily lives despite the various challenges, including difficulty finding resonance with a particular practice, the complexity or intensity of its demands, and limited time. The tips and guidance provided are designed to make spiritual practice a part of one's life in an accessible and sustainable manner.

Incorporating spiritual practice into our daily lives can be thorny, but there are many ways to make it work. For instance, you could commit to a short period of mindfulness each day or take a few moments before bed to reflect quietly. However, only some have the luxury of having a dedicated space for their spiritual practice. Hence, you may need to experiment with different approaches depending on your lifestyle and constraints. Furthermore, although it may take courage to be open about your beliefs, talking about them can also help build stronger connections with those around you, which is a crucial part of any spiritual journey.

Here are some ideas that might help you fully embody and integrate your chosen spiritual path into your life:

- **Do some research on your spiritual practice.** Take your spiritual practice to the next level by researching its history and origins. Delve deeper into its traditions and customs to gain an even greater understanding of it. This foundation can serve as the basis for further learning and exploration. Additionally, you could look up facts related to your spiritual practice that illustrate how they are connected, deepening your appreciation of the subject.

- **Look for a teacher or mentor.** Seeking out a teacher or mentor can be beneficial for spiritual growth. A mentor can offer wisdom, insights, and support that often comes with life experience. They can guide how to apply the teachings in everyday life. Answer any questions that might arise. Plus, help you stay motivated despite the challenges encountered on the journey. Mentors are also great resources for ideas and techniques that could make your journey smoother and more successful.

- **Find a support group.** Connecting with a like-minded community is an excellent way to seek spiritual guidance and support. Joining a support group can help you form relationships with people who share your values, such as love, and become more mindful of what matters in life. Additionally, it enables you to focus on relationships, which leads to greater well-being rather than fear. By connecting with others who hold similar beliefs, you can gain valuable wisdom and understanding. One way to connect with like-minded individuals is by joining virtual groups or attending local meetups dedicated to exploring spirituality. Virtual groups on social media platforms like Facebook provide a convenient way to interact with others who share your interests. Then, local meetups close to where you live or work can save you time and alleviate travel stress. These events offer an opportunity to build relationships with people who share your interests, allowing you to learn from each other's experiences and share advice, stories, and reflections. You can also use these gatherings as a chance to rest and relax away from the hustle and bustle of everyday life.

Making spiritual practice a daily habit will help you integrate it as a significant and essential aspect of your life. At first, you might not be able to do this, but that is okay. As you become accustomed to it, start slowly, then increase the time each day.

Embodying spiritual practices can be a powerful way to cultivate mental, emotional, and physical well-being. Every religion or spiritual ritual provides a unique set of practices that can bring harmony into one's life. For example, meditation has been an ancient practice for centuries to promote peace, clarity, and connection. Additionally, mindfulness activities have become popular tools for reducing stress and anxiety. Meanwhile, yoga helps to build strength and flexibility in the body. Integrating such spirituality into your daily routine can provide immense benefits when living a fulfilling life.

Crafting a meaningful and satisfying spiritual path is essential to your life's journey. Awareness of this importance can help guide your decisions and help you stay connected to your spirituality no matter what. Even if you do not have that connection immediately, looking after other aspects of yourself should be the first step. Besides, many struggle with feeling guilty about self-care before caring for those around them. Yet, remorse would not benefit anyone in the long run. To create an enriched experience when cultivating spirituality, explore new perspectives, and embrace various faith-related activities. Further, enrich your journey by discovering historical information and reading scripture related to your beliefs. This way, you can strengthen your understanding and appreciation of faith.

Below are some tips for getting in touch with your spirituality.

- **Take a moment to include spirituality in your daily routine.** Meditate, reflect, or pray for five minutes each day. Alternatively, consider taking a few minutes during a break or transition period for those with busier schedules to connect with your spiritual side. For example, take a few deep breaths and center yourself before starting a task, or practice mindfulness while doing a mundane activity like washing dishes. Every little moment counts towards cultivating a more spiritual mindset. Likewise, connecting with your spiritual side is invaluable, as incorporating spiritual mindfulness into your life gives greater inner peace and satisfaction.

- **Explore any religious traditions from your upbringing.** Think about the beliefs instilled in you during childhood and how others viewed these practices. Reflect on your lessons from past experiences and investigate how they impact your decisions today. Also, recognize commonalities and differences between personal beliefs and practices, with those of other people who share a similar background as you. Take time to learn about different cultures, their values, traditions, and ways of living that could be integral to understanding yourself better. Discovering your spiritual self will allow you to grow in knowledge and empathy toward others.

6

Three Shamanic Worlds

People often discuss their curiosity and desire to explore the unknown, particularly to embark on a journey into the 'lower world.' But what does that mean? Are we talking about an overseas trip or something entirely different? From a scientific perspective, this realm may not even exist. Yet there are still many who choose to pursue this mysterious quest.

In visiting such a place, a brave adventuring spirit and an imaginative approach to your travels are needed. Plus, you will uncover new sites and stories on our journey, which can be an incredible experience. Likewise, you may even find yourself learning something unexpected along the way. But first, let us explore what these mysterious realms are.

Lower World

Daydreaming and meditation can open the door to a realm often considered the 'lower world.' In this altered state, you can become an animal spirit, immerse yourself in the lower world, and explore what lies beneath the surface. Picture yourself as a spirit animal inhabiting a realm of hills and valleys, with lakes and rivers that seem oddly reminiscent of your hometown. Behold its ancient inhabitants, creatures existing since before humans ever inhabited Earth. In this hidden land, you can observe these beings engaging in activities and forming families or tribes. *What kind of food do they eat? What type of attire do they wear? How have these creatures developed a form of governance, and how does it respond to their environment?*

These questions are more than just academic musings; the answers can reveal powerful insights into the relationship between humankind and nature. As such, *do they use some technology? Can they communicate telepathically or by speaking aloud? What kind of games do they play together, and what music do they enjoy listening to? How do they craft their instruments, and if technology is employed, how does it impact them?* Through exploring such questions, you will understand more about the lower world.

For those who have never ventured to the lower world, it can be helpful to imagine descending into a cave, entering the water, or even slipping into slumber to access this mysterious realm. Awaiting your arrival, this peculiar realm is like nothing you have encountered before; it features a stunning yet barren landscape of hot and gritty terrain dotted with swirling clouds of dust and sand. There is no sign of life, with no animals or trees in sight. Not even lush greenery or fresh streams. Instead, this desolate domain is characterized by a vast expanse that provokes your senses while fueling your creativity. As you traverse its unforgiving surroundings, uncover hidden oases, rocky outcroppings, and ancient ruins that offer a glimpse into the culture and customs of the ancestors living in this realm.

Entering the lower world is much like stepping into a dream that is more vibrant and authentic than reality. As such, you are conscious of being in an environment removed from the physical realm but have access to the guidance of your ancestors. Messages and insights arise from this unique landscape, offering insight into how to navigate life's challenges. Rituals and ceremonies can bring healing and transformation on multiple levels. All of this speaks to a deeply spiritual experience that fosters growth and understanding beyond what is tangible and visible. Thus, the lower realm is a rich and enigmatic environment, allowing shamans to seek out the wisdom of the spirit world and utilize it to benefit their communities. It is believed that within these depths lies ancient knowledge used by generations of ancestors for centuries. Not only does this provide a deeper understanding of the past, but it also gives great insight into possible paths for the future. Each journey taken by a shaman into this realm can bring fresh perspectives and challenges, yielding invaluable treasures that are sure to be shared for ages.

Middle World

The middle world is a rich and expansive landscape containing the physical elements of plants and animals, weather patterns, human communities, and the more ethereal realms of spiritual energy. Shamans use this multifaceted world to service their work while making regular journeys between the upper and lower worlds. This middle world profoundly permeates human life, affecting our ability to connect and the environment. Likewise, it shapes our mindsets and informs our physical universe. A greater understanding of this deep layer of reality can bring positive life changes.

In the shamanic view, this world differs from mainstream science in that it does not distinguish between living and non-living matter or animate beings with consciousness like ourselves and other living beings without consciousness. It also does not separate humans from nature. The middle world is the physical world we inhabit and much more. For example, plants, animals, and weather systems interact with each other to create a complex web of life. Humans are part of this larger ecosystem, adding our human perspective to the mix. Looking around us can give clues about how we fit into this environment. What we see in our yards or the palms of our hands reflects and influences the interconnectedness of everything in this middle world.

Aside from that, the middle world is a complex realm of physical, mental, and spiritual energies. It incorporates the natural forces of animals, plants, weather patterns, and human-created communities and cultures. Here shamans work their magic to heal others or themselves through their bodies and minds by tapping into these energies directly. In addition to shamans, modern energy medicine practitioners believe that this middle world holds powerful forces that can be harnessed in healing practices such as Reiki, chakra balancing, qigong, acupuncture, and more. These techniques seek to restore balance and harmony within an individual's body for personal healing and to release negative or blocked energy for overall wellness.

Connections to spiritual realms, such as the upper and lower worlds, are made in the middle world. It is also a place of energetic intersection, where we can find our way to healing by interacting with its components: *plants, animals, humans and even rocks or stones.* Understanding how to work with the energies of this middle world can help us achieve greater health and happiness in our lives. The shamanic practice involves engaging with the middle world on both physical and non-physical levels so that we may gain insight through spiritual journeying and vision quests. Navigating this realm is essential to unlocking its potential for growth and transformation.

Upper World

The Upper World is believed to be a place of spiritual and divine realms, and it can be accessed through meditation and shamanic practices. Some describe it as a realm above us, beyond the physical world, while others may envision it as a dimension or alternate reality. Regardless of its description, the Upper World is where individuals can connect with higher beings. However, not only does this land offer an ethereal connection to seek guidance from entities such as teachers or wise ones. Yet, it is believed to provide access to knowledge that cannot be found elsewhere. Moreover, this higher realm contains portals that connect one's earthly life with destiny in other domains.

Likewise, the upper world is a land of magic and mystery, where you can meet and converse with a divine pantheon of gods, goddesses, and ancestors. To access the spirit realm, you must journey through dreams or meditation, enabling you to explore various planes of existence. Some are more tangible than others, but all are inhabited by beings that serve as tutors. These beings can show you how to discover your true purpose in life and help expand your knowledge of both the spiritual and earthly realms. Furthermore, they can provide essential insights into how the two intersect and influence each other.

When looking to receive wisdom and advice, the upper world is an ideal place to seek it. This realm comprises three distinct components: the sky world populated by heavenly beings, the land(s) above, home to many passed spiritual teachers and Earth itself. Interestingly, this is not just a place for guidance but also a source of powerful energy that can be tapped into. By journeying up to this higher realm, you can unlock hidden knowledge, discover ancient secrets and be aided in your work as a shaman.

Pillar 4

Connection

Pillar four of shamanism delves into connecting with the spiritual world through altered states of consciousness. This includes dreams, out-of-body experiences, astral projection, and drumming and chanting as tools to establish this connection. Lucid dreaming has also been explored as an additional form of altered state to explore this deeper connection. Additionally, many shamans believe fasting and prolonged periods of silence can further allow for opportunities to connect with the spirit world. By cultivating these techniques, you can deeply understand your shared spiritual journey.

7

Dreams

*H*ave you ever stopped to consider the mysteries of dreaming? What lies beneath our conscious minds while we are
asleep? Do dreams have hidden meanings or are they simply random thoughts? These questions, and more, have perplexed
us since the beginning of time. Here are some answers to the que-
ries posed a while ago, with a few extra musings thrown in for
good measure.

What Are Dreams

Dreams provide a great window into our innermost thoughts and
feelings. While most dreams are experienced as incomprehensi-
ble and bizarre, many are vivid and powerful, in either black and
white or color. These images may contain symbols that represent
our fears, hopes, aspirations, or desires. Scientists believe that
dreaming helps us process difficult emotions and experiences by
making sense of the information we take during our waking life.
Additionally, journaling has been used for centuries to capture a
snapshot of the dreamer's inner landscape at any given moment,
providing valuable insight into our subconscious minds.

When dreaming, it can be in various colors and shapes, from pas-
tel hues to technicolor scenes. During the rapid eye movement
(REM) stage of sleep, dreams occur as our brain activity is similar

to its activity while awake but with certain deviations. Also, it is worth noting that this phase is fundamental for memory retention and learning processes, hence why getting optimum periods of restful sleep is essential. Furthermore, people tend to have different dreams on the same night, color or black-and-white, depending on their state of mind. All in all, there is not just one definitive way to dream; everyone experiences it differently.

Under REM sleep, your brain processes and stores information you have taken during the day while also helping you consolidate memories. You can have trouble recalling things if you do not get enough of this stage in the sleep cycle. As such, dreaming is thought to help process and regulate emotional experiences, allowing emotions and memories to be sorted into meaningful categories. This could explain why it sometimes feels like we can never fully capture a dream's details when we attempt to recount them upon waking. Rapid eye movement occurs in bursts throughout the night, with the most vivid dreaming occurring near morning.

Hence, everyone can dream, but only some can recall their dreams. While some people can vividly remember their nighttime visions, others may have no memory. Personal experiences shape dreams, so the memories will be distinct even if two people share the same dream. As such, exploring these dreamscapes can give us a better understanding of ourselves and how we interact with the world.

Out of Body Experience

An out-of-body experience, or OBE, is a phenomenon in which a person feels like they have left their physical body and are observing the world from an external point of view. During an OBE, individuals may see their body from a third-person perspective, feel like they are flying, or even travel to other realms beyond the physical world. The subjective experience of an OBE can differ from person to person, with some reporting feelings of weightlessness or tingling and others experiencing intense emotions or a sense of enlightenment.

One theory suggests that OBEs are caused by a malfunction in the brain, specifically the parietal lobe. For the integration of sensory data and the development of self-awareness, the parietal lobe is in charge. During an OBE, the parietal lobe malfunctions, creating the illusion of leaving the body. Studies that identified alterations in brain activity during OBEs support this notion. Another theory is that OBEs are extrasensory perceptions that allow people to see beyond the physical world. This theory suggests that OBEs are humans' natural ability to perceive the world beyond their physical body. Some proponents of this theory believe that OBEs result from the soul or spirit leaving the physical body and traveling to other planes of existence.

While OBEs can be transformative experiences, they can also be unsettling or dangerous for some people. If you are trying to induce one, you should be cautious and seek the right advice when approaching them. Discussing concerns with a healthcare professional is essential, as some medical conditions or medications can increase the likelihood of an OBE. Also, various means can induce an OBE, such as meditation, sleep deprivation, hypnosis, and certain drugs like ketamine or DMT. These methods are often used by individuals seeking to induce an OBE intentionally. However, it is essential to note that inducing an OBE intentionally can be risky and should only be attempted by experienced practitioners.

The subjective experience of an OBE can differ from person to person. Some individuals report feelings of weightlessness or tingling, while others experience intense emotions or a sense of enlightenment. Many people describe their OBE as a spiritual or mystical experience; some even report communication with spiritual beings or guides. In fact, OBEs are often associated with spiritual or metaphysical practices like shamanism or new-age beliefs. As such, some individuals with OBEs report a newfound sense of spirituality or a shift in their worldview. Others may feel unsettled or confused by their experience, particularly if they need a framework for understanding it.

Clairvoyant Abilities

Throughout history, clairvoyant abilities have been the source of much mystery and debate. While some believe they result from spiritual or supernatural influence, others argue that it is simply an extension of normal senses. Clairvoyance can also manifest itself in various ways, such as seeing images in the mind's eye or feeling strongly about a particular topic. Those with these gifts may be able to identify potential dangers before they occur or pinpoint the location of missing persons. In addition, some people may even claim to receive messages from the spirit world through dreams or visions. Although not everyone believes in this form of perception, many still find it fascinating.

Many clairvoyants claim that their experiences are uncontrollable and that they have little or no control over when or how they happen. They could experience unexpected epiphanies or get messages in their dreams. Others experience physical feelings like a sharp chill or tingling in their limbs. Meanwhile, some clairvoyants have even reported hearing voices or seeing visuals that seem to originate from somewhere else.

There is no one-size-fits-all technique for improving clairvoyant powers because developing these abilities is sometimes a personal experience. While some people may have a natural propensity for clairvoyance, others may need more effort to hone their skills over time. Developing clairvoyant talents could benefit from methods like energy work, visualization, and meditation. It is also helpful to contact other spiritualists or clairvoyants who can provide advice and assistance.

Moreover, it is essential to note that while clairvoyant abilities are often associated with psychics or mediums, they are not limited to these professions. Many people possess clairvoyant abilities without even realizing it, and they may experience glimpses of the unseen without consciously acknowledging them. Additionally, some clairvoyants choose not to use their powers for psychic readings or other forms of divination but to enhance their spiritual journeys or connect with loved ones who have passed on.

One common use of clairvoyant abilities is communicating with deceased loved ones. Many people who have lost someone close to them report feeling a sense of ongoing connection and may experience visions or other sensory input that they interpret as signs from their loved ones. While there is no scientific proof of an afterlife or the ability to communicate with the dead, many people find comfort in these experiences, which may offer a sense of continuity and connection even after death.

Clairvoyant abilities are a fascinating and often misunderstood aspect of the human experience. While there is no "right" way to experience clairvoyance, many people report seeing things beyond the physical realm, which can provide great comfort and insight. Whether through meditation, energy work, or simply being open to the possibilities, anyone can develop their clairvoyant abilities and gain a deeper understanding of the world around them.

Energetic Vibrations

Energetic vibrations refer to the energy movement in and around us. This energy makes up our physical and emotional states and can be impacted by external factors such as sound, light, and the energy of others. Many people believe that our energetic vibrations can also affect our perception of reality, including our experiences during out-of-body experiences.

The vibrational state often associated with OBEs can be described as a buzzing or humming sensation throughout the body. It may feel like an intense surge of energy flowing through the body, causing a tingling sensation or even full-body vibrations. This state can be extreme and overwhelming, but it is often a sign that the individual is about to enter an altered state of consciousness.

As mentioned earlier, the experience of the vibrational state during an OBE can be different for each person. Some individuals may see themselves from a third-person perspective, while others may feel like they are floating or being pulled out through their head or chest area. An individual's energetic vibration can also influence these experiences. Several things, such as our ideas, emotions, and physical state, might affect the energetic vibration of our body. If we feel low or negative, our energetic vibration may be lower, impacting our perception of ourselves during an OBE. On the other hand, if we feel positive and confident, our energetic vibration may be higher, allowing us to perceive ourselves as more empowered and secure.

In many spiritual and metaphysical practices, energetic vibration is crucial in achieving spiritual growth and connecting with higher states of consciousness. By raising our energetic vibration through techniques such as meditation, visualization, and energy healing, we can access higher states of consciousness and unlock the full potential of our spiritual selves. Also, energetic vibrations play a significant role in our experiences during out-of-body experiences. While the vibrational state during an OBE can be intense and overwhelming, it can also be a powerful tool for exploring different states of consciousness and connecting with our spiritual selves. Understanding how our energetic vibration affects our perception of reality, we can work towards raising our vibration and unlocking the full potential of our spiritual selves.

Astral Projection

Astral projection, also known as *"astral travel,"* is a phenomenon where a person feels they have left their physical body and can explore the world around them from an outside perspective. It is frequently described as a feeling of consciousness outside the body.

While the concept of astral projection may seem far-fetched, many spiritual traditions, such as Buddhism and Taoism, have explored the possibilities of astral projection for thousands of years. For instance, Hindu tradition includes the concept of the *"subtle body,"* which comprises various layers of energy or consciousness that extend beyond the physical body. Similarly, Theosophy teaches about the existence of an *"astral body,"* which can be separated from the physical body during astral projection.

Besides Buddhism and Taoism, many other spiritual traditions have explored the possibilities of astral projection, including Sufism, Kabbalah, and Hermeticism. In some cases, astral projection is viewed as a spiritual growth and enlightenment tool. Meanwhile, in others, it is seen as a means of accessing hidden knowledge or communicating with spiritual beings. Today, many people use astral projection for personal growth, spiritual exploration, relaxation, and stress relief.

One technique for achieving astral projection is deep relaxation. Many people use exercises like progressive relaxation or a body scan, which involves focusing on each part of the body, from the toes to the head, and releasing any tension. Once the body is deeply relaxed, the individual can focus on their consciousness and mental state. Visualization is another technique commonly used for astral projection. One popular method is to imagine yourself climbing a rope or a ladder out of your body or drifting upwards like a balloon. Another technique is to visualize yourself in a favorite location or alternate reality. The more vivid the visualization, the better the chance of inducing an astral projection.

During astral projection, people feel like they are flying or floating. Likewise, they may be able to interact with their environment, including the physical world or planes of existence. Some people see deceased loved ones, spirit guides, or other entities that may be present in the astral realm. These interactions can take many forms, such as conversations, receiving guidance or messages, or even receiving healing energy.

Yet, these experiences are highly subjective and can vary greatly from person to person. While some may have vivid and life-changing experiences during astral projection, others may not have any experience at all. Moreover, like any altered state of consciousness, astral projection is not without its risks. As such, many people report feeling disoriented or exhausted after the experience. Meanwhile, others have reported encountering negative entities or spirits. Hence, taking the necessary precautions before attempting astral projection, like grounding oneself before and after the practice and protecting oneself with spiritual or energetic shields, is essential.

Visions of Deceased Loved Ones

Many people struggle to find comfort and closure after the death of a loved one, and some turn to shamanic practices to help them connect with their loved ones beyond the grave. In shamanic practices, visions of deceased loved ones have shared experiences that are believed to offer guidance and healing to the living. In shamanic traditions, visions of deceased loved ones are believed to be a way of connecting with the spiritual world.

Experiences of seeing deceased loved ones can be a powerful way to reconnect with them and feel their presence. Such encounters may bridge the gap between the material and spiritual realms, providing profound insights into life and its purpose. It is believed that these visions are not random occurrences but rather intentional messages from the spirit world, where loved ones remain aware of our lives, intentions, and struggles. They offer guidance, comfort, or even warnings to help us journey. Likewise, they may provide insight into our past decisions or current situations.

Shamans interpret these messages and offer advice on integrating them into the individual's life. It may be a means of solace and resolution for some. For others, it can be a way of continuing a relationship with a loved one who has passed on.

However, not all visions of our departed loved ones are trustworthy or beneficial. Some may arise from intense grief, anguish, or other mental issues, while societal norms or media depictions could impact others. As such, approach these situations with judgment and clarity. Shamanic practices often involve visions of deceased family members providing spiritual advice and solace. Additionally, research into near-death experiences reveals that many people report having a spiritual encounter with their beloved ones when facing a life-threatening situation. Therefore, it appears that these visions can offer comfort in a dire situation regardless of culture or religion.

Each person has different experiences in intensity, frequency, and length. Although not scientifically proven, they offer comfort and solace to those who have lost loved ones, providing a sense of continuity and connection even after death. While not all visions may be genuine or beneficial, it is necessary to approach these experiences with an open mind and discernment.

Lucid Dreams

Shamanic journeys and lucid dreaming are closely linked. In fact, many shamans believe that the experience of lucid dreaming is a form of direct access to the spirit world. During a lucid dream, asking questions, receiving answers from spirit guides, and exploring unknown realms of knowledge and intuition is possible. Furthermore, lucid dreamers can also use their dreams to improve physical health or confront personal fears. All these aspects show how shamanic experiences can be enhanced with an awareness of lucid dreaming.

Besides, lucid dreaming is an incredible skill, allowing you to explore a world of limitless possibilities. With lucid dreams, you can fly to distant galaxies and experience sensations that do not exist in the physical realm. Furthermore, some have used lucid dreams as an effective tool for getting insights into their subconscious minds, such as working through challenging problems or becoming better at something through virtual practice. In addition, research suggests that lucid dreams contribute to improved mental well-being due to the sense of empowerment they generate.

Likewise, lucid dreaming offers unique opportunities for exploration and emotional healing. The activity allows us to safely process our feelings and thoughts without turning to harmful behaviors such as drug abuse or self-harm. With patience and dedication, we can dive into the mysterious realm of lucid dreams and discover new opportunities for self-exploration and personal growth. In fact, lucid dreaming has resulted in various experiences, such as overcoming nightmares or enhancing creativity. However, lucid dreaming can carry certain risks, such as sleep deprivation, false awakenings, and sleep paralysis, which may require extra knowledge and care. Lucid dreaming can also be induced through various methods, including reality checks, *mnemonic induction of lucid dreams (MILD)*, and *wake-initiated lucid dreaming (WILD)*, providing a range of options for individuals to choose from.

Mnemonic induction of lucid dreams (MILD) involves intending to remember that you are dreaming while falling asleep. This is usually done by repeating a phrase, like *"I will recognize that I am dreaming,"* repeatedly until falling asleep. The idea is that eventually, this phrase will become so ingrained in your subconscious that it will carry over into your dream, allowing you to become lucid. Meanwhile, although most people think of lucid dreams as occurring while asleep, it is possible to have a lucid dream while awake. This type of experience is the *wake-induced lucid dream (WILD)*. As such, it involves maintaining consciousness as your body falls asleep, allowing you to enter a dream state while remaining aware. For instance, this method can be done by lying still and focusing on a single thought, such as a swirling pattern, until you eventually become lucid in the dream.

Besides that, meditation can be an effective way to improve your lucid dreaming ability and overall well-being. It helps focus, relax, and be mindful in the present moment. This mindfulness enables you to be aware of your thoughts and feelings at night, allowing you to process them more efficiently so that the intrusive worries that aim to keep you awake during the night become less frequent. Additionally, meditation reduces stress levels, which are known to cause insomnia. Consequently, it may benefit individuals struggling with such sleeping problems as they will experience deeper and more restful sleep.

With lucid dreaming, you can control and bend your dream environment to your will. Whether you explore a city where animals converse or embark on an interstellar journey with an alien companion, your mind can craft any adventure imaginable. Beyond mere wonderment, dreams can also become terrifying if you find yourself face-to-face with monsters or strange dreamscapes that seem too surreal for reality. For thousands of years, various cultures have harnessed the power of lucid dreaming to uncover hidden insights into their personal lives and understanding of the universe.

Altogether, lucid dreaming allows you to explore your imagination in ways that would be impossible in the real world. Not only can you travel to distant planets and explore new and exciting places, but you can also meet characters from your dreams which can become friends or companions. Beyond this, lucid dreaming also has practical applications. For example, it can help reduce stress and increase relaxation, making it a helpful tool for those looking to manage their mental health. Additionally, lucid dreaming is surprisingly straightforward and accessible to anyone looking to get started. This makes it an attractive option for shamans seeking personal growth or insight into their spiritual practice.

8

Trance

Trance is an altered state of consciousness characterized by heightened awareness and receptivity to spiritual communication. It can be induced through meditation, hypnosis, yoga, prayer, dancing, chanting, or rhythmic music. This state of mind also offers a deeper insight into oneself and potential access to higher wisdom. By engaging in trance-like forms, often called astral projection, one can traverse the realms of divination and intuition to understand one's life path and purpose better.

Altered State of Consciousness

A subjective experience, distinct from everyday consciousness, is known as an Altered State of Consciousness (ASC). It can be heightened awareness and focus on one's internal and external experiences. Various techniques can induce ASCs, such as meditation, hypnosis, or sensory deprivation (e.g., floating in water). Certain drugs or psychedelics may also alter consciousness, although the effects vary greatly depending on the substance and dose. Understanding brainwave patterns associated with ASCs could also provide insight into their nature.

Moreover, altered states of consciousness can involve changes in a person's perception and emotions and a sense of temporal distortion. While in an ASC, individuals may experience reality differently, leading to new insights into their surroundings and fostering heightened creativity. Furthermore, recent studies have suggested that these ASCs can be therapeutically for depression or addiction.

To fully comprehend what happens in our brain during an ASC, you must understand the everyday scientific processes of our neural network. Our brains rely on electricity to send messages between neurons and activate muscles, enabled by chemicals called neurotransmitters. These neurotransmitters are small molecules produced by neurons that act as messengers and travel across synapses, narrowing gaps between neighboring cells. When these neurotransmitters bind with receptors on the receiving cell, it triggers electrical signals within the connected neuron(s). Depending on the type of receptor it binds with, it can either activate or inhibit activity in both cells' membranes, allowing them to travel through nerve networks throughout our bodies. During an altered state of consciousness (ASC), different reactions can occur in the brain due to changes in this process, such as increased levels of certain neurotransmitters influencing receptor stimulation.

Subsequently, it is believed that people in ASC have a deeper understanding of themselves and the world around them, enabling them to gain insights into some of life's most difficult questions. As such, when the mind enters a state of heightened awareness, we can often connect with the subconscious on a deeper level, unlocking new perspectives and creativity. For instance, many famous artists have used techniques to influence their consciousness to create some of their most iconic works. From the colorful paintings of Vincent van Gogh to the psychedelic sounds of the Beatles, altered states have played a major role in the creative process of many artists throughout history. Likewise, ASC has also been linked to self-reflection and a greater self-understanding. By introspecting on one's thoughts and emotions, we may address deep-seated personal issues, leading to greater self-awareness and personal growth.

Many people experience altered states of consciousness, often without being aware of it. This can happen when we are so engrossed in a movie or book that we forget where we are or during meditation when our minds wander off. Or have you ever noticed moments of clarity when time slows down and you feel connected to the world? Lots of people experience this type of altered state. The indicators of altered consciousness can include vivid imagery, heightened emotionality, absence of fear, and even feeling part of something bigger than oneself. Understanding the signs and symptoms associated with these altered conditions allows us to gain insight into our experiences and those around us. These details are detailed in the book and provide invaluable insights into new realms of self-awareness.

Drumming

Drumming has been a significant part of religious ceremonies for centuries, serving various purposes depending on the specific tradition. In shamanic rituals, drums are often used for healing, divination, and communicating with the spirit world. The use of drums can vary greatly depending on the culture, with different beats and rhythms used to evoke specific emotions or symbolize certain ideas.

In some religions, drumming is seen to connect with the divine and our inner selves, with the beating of the drum representing the heartbeat that connects us all. Certain sounds or vibrations produced by the drum can also have a special symbolism in specific religious ceremonies, such as the summoning of ancestors or deities.

Shamans use drums in ceremonies to communicate with spirits and ancestors who are not present. During shamanic ceremonies, specific spirits may be summoned to aid with healing or protection from harmful spirits.

The sound of the drum has been used in many cultures worldwide for thousands of years, often as a means of spiritual healing and connection with the divine. Drumming is believed to create an opening in the subconscious that can allow practitioners to access altered states of consciousness and gain insight into their innermost thoughts and feelings. Native American tribes traditionally used drums in ceremonial rituals to invoke powerful spirits for spiritual guidance. In modern times, drum circles are often seen as a way to connect with nature, gather good luck, and promote emotional well-being. Additionally, therapeutic drumming is beneficial for increased relaxation and relief from physical pain, mental illness, and emotional trauma.

In addition to drumming, other percussion instruments like rattles, bells, and chimes are often used in shamanic ceremonies. These instruments add texture and depth to the drum sound, often creating a sonic landscape that the shaman and participants can navigate.

Overall, the sound of the drum is a critical component of shamanic ceremonies, and it is believed to have a powerful impact on the psyche and the spirit. The steady, rhythmic beat of the drum can be a powerful tool for inducing an altered state of consciousness, connecting with the spiritual world, and accessing hidden knowledge and wisdom.

Rattles

The rattle has been a part of humanity for millennia. As such, archaeological discoveries revealed that these objects were used in ceremonial activities dating back to 3000 BCE. They were typically crafted from animal skins stretched over wooden or gourd shells with small seeds that produce sounds when shaken. Initially used for music-making, rattles were regarded as having supernatural powers. Likewise, they were believed to chase away evil spirits and attract positive energy.

In shamanistic traditions, rattles were used to induce trance states and call forth spirits during rituals. The vibrations generated by this instrument pave the way for an altered state of awareness that allows humans and spirits to bridge the gap between them. Apart from their musical and spiritual purposes, rattles were also used for other activities. For instance, shamans frequently incorporated rattles into their healing practices; some were explicitly designed for this purpose. With a rattle containing herbs, the shaman would shake it over the person's body, spreading the herbs and their healing properties on their skin. As such, the sound of shaking these rattles was believed to help drive away evil spirits who might be causing sickness in someone's life or body, making them better again.

Furthermore, rattles were used to connect to the spirit world, assisting individuals in exploring visions and gaining knowledge of their ancestors. They guide their rhythmic vibrations, and the sound produced can be meditative, helping those involved to focus on their meditations without the distraction of external noise. Additionally, rattles are often used in various religious ceremonies, such as purifying and blessing rituals. In some cultures, rattles are believed to bring luck or protection when hung over doorways or placed under beds.

Rattle-making is a traditional craft worldwide, and the process can vary widely. In Native American tribes, rattles were often made with added feathers to symbolize the connection between spirits and humans. Moreover, Latin America is known for its distinctively loud-sounding rattles. Elsewhere, in Northern Europe's Sami community, rattles are crafted from reindeer hooves. Meanwhile, Chinese culture uses bells as a type of rattle for warding off evil spirits.

To make a rattle, do the following steps:

1. Cut two pieces of leather or animal skin into circular shapes. The size and shape of your circle can vary depending on your preference.
2. Place the two pieces of leather together with the smooth sides facing inwards.
3. Using a needle and thread, stitch around the outer edge of the circle, leaving a small opening to add the filling.
4. Once you have left an opening in your circle, add the small stones, beans, or seeds into the pocket created by the leather.
5. After adding the filling, continue sewing around the outer edge of the circle until it is completely closed.
6. Cut a small piece of leather or string and stitch it to the top of the circle to create a handle.
7. OPTIONAL: Decorate your rattle, and attach any beads, feathers, or other decorative items using glue, thread, or wire.

With these steps complete, you have your unique rattle that can be used during spiritual practices or music production. Rattles can be made with various materials depending on cultural traditions. Hence, you can create a unique rattle that aligns with your preferences and practices.

Ecstatic Dancing

Ecstatic dance is a form of shamanic healing practiced for thousands of years. It involves deep introspection, physical exertion, and intense concentration, which requires gradual increases in difficulty as the practitioner continues to train. During these exercises, practitioners are encouraged to use visualization to find balance and control over their movements. Furthermore, ecstatic dancing can be used for its therapeutic benefits, allowing individuals to gain clarity in thought patterns and strengthen their connection with themselves and their environment.

In shamanic healing, ecstatic dancing can heal individuals suffering from physical or mental illness. The idea behind this method is that movement helps release negative energy from within the body, both physically and spiritually, allowing positive energy to flow freely once again. In fact, it is possible to communicate with the divine by dancing as a form of meditation. Additionally, it can aid in your recovery and increase your inner peace. Depending on what you need, you can do it by yourself or with others. Shamanistic rituals such as ecstatic dancing demand many participants. It strains your body and forces you to tune with your spirit, mind, and body.

To be a successful ecstatic dancer, having the right mindset is vital. With a combination of self-focus and concentration on others around you, it is possible to immerse yourself in the experience and find joy in movement. While it may take some time to get accustomed to this form of dance, the effort is worth it as it strengthens your physical and mental health. To improve safety, starting slowly and gradually increasing your stamina is essential; beginning with short yet intense sessions can help you reach the desired results without overexerting yourself. Ecstatic dancing is an incredible way to open up and express yourself without judgment or restrictions.

Get your body ready for more intense exercises by doing light warm-ups such as walking or stretching. Then, challenge yourself with activities like jogging in place or jumping jacks. Both exercises can help increase your heart rate and build muscle tone. Aim for three minutes of jogging in place and four minutes of jumping jacks. Additionally, it is essential to stay hydrated throughout your workout, and allowing yourself rest breaks when necessary is critical.

Ecstatic dance training often begins with learning how to breathe correctly and releasing any tension in the body. To help you do this, try this simple breathing exercise:

1. Sit or stand comfortably, close your eyes, and relax.
2. Take a few deep breaths, exhaling through your mouth after each.
3. Breathe slowly through both nostrils, filling your lungs with air before exhaling slowly through one nostril at a time.
4. Repeat the process by breathing out through both nostrils together (equalizing).
5. Do this three times per day for five minutes at a time until it becomes automatic for you.

Besides that, dancing is a captivating form of expression, emphasizing flow and emotion. It encourages movements that often feel spontaneous but comes from your internal drive. To truly tap into this art form, embrace the music while simultaneously syncing up with your partner or group. This combination goes a long way in creating an unforgettable experience. Also, as you let yourself free in the moment, let the music guide you while being aware of how each body part moves in unison with each other and the surrounding objects. Through this process, new dimensions of creative expression can be explored.

As you dance, focus on your breath and visualize your goal. For example, if you are having trouble controlling the movements of your arms and legs, focus on them instead of letting them flail about aimlessly. You may even want to imagine an invisible string attached to each limb that controls its movements; this way, you can focus on managing those strings rather than worrying about what others think of your dancing style.

However, learning to dance ecstatically is about more than just mastering the moves and techniques. As such, it is also about connecting with your own body. That said, relaxing and letting go of any worries about making mistakes is important. At the same time, proper breathing and tension release practices are essential for building up the strength and stamina required for more complex movements like spinning or jumping. With practice and patience, anyone can gain confidence in their ecstatic dancing ability.

Chanting

Chanting is an ancient practice with many varied purposes. From helping to ground oneself and find clarity of mind to connecting with spiritual guides and tapping into higher wisdom, chanting has been used for millennia. Whether used in a solitary or shared setting, this powerful tool can bring about profound changes in those who participate. In addition, using chanting as a form of meditation can greatly benefit the practitioner's well-being, allowing them to relax and connect with their inner self. With so much potential for transformation, it is no wonder chanting has stood the test of time.

By reciting mantras, one can bring positive energy into their lives and manifest the change they seek in terms of better relationships, improved health, or achieving goals. For instance, chanting "I am loved" or "I have courage" can help boost self-esteem and reduce negative emotions such as anger and fear. Additionally, chanting can help increase resilience, decrease stress, and enhance concentration. Ultimately, this age-old practice is a powerful way to cultivate inner peace and foster meaningful connections.

Aside from that, chanting can be a powerful tool for self-transformation through its ability to unlock mental and spiritual blocks, elevate the mind into higher states of consciousness, and provide profound insights. This practice has been used by spiritual seekers around the world, from ancient cultures to modern religions. Reflective chants can help you achieve inner peace and greater clarity, improving physical health and mental well-being. As a form of meditation and prayer, chanting has been known to foster feelings of unity and connectedness with something larger than oneself. Ultimately, it is a simple but effective way to transform yourself on your path of spiritual growth.

When selecting the sounds you want to chant, you have a key responsibility. Selecting what resonates with you is about your taste and preference and which sounds speak to your consciousness the most at that moment. Remember, only you can make this choice. For example, if someone has cancer and feels exhausted, I might recommend toning instead of chanting. Binaural beats can promote relaxation by working with brainwave frequencies and calming the mind and body. As such, listening to binaural beats can be an effective way to alter the mind's neural networks to reduce stress hormones, which can then help facilitate natural healing processes within the body.

Furthermore, binaural beats can be experienced through headphones at night while in bed or even during meditation sessions throughout the day for a more focused healing experience. Overall, chanting is a powerful tool for connecting with the deeper parts of our being and understanding the world around us. It allows us to access more profound levels of knowledge, tapping into otherwise inaccessible energies. Furthermore, it can align our thoughts, emotions, and intentions to manifest desired outcomes. Adding a factual component to this technique, chanting often follows established patterns or rhymes based on tradition, aiding practitioners in pursuing enlightenment and connection with nature. Finally, whatever type of chanting resonates best with you is always the right choice.

Entheogens

Entheogens have had a long-standing legacy across many cultures and religions worldwide, from Ancient Greece to Egypt, where they were known as the *"food of the gods,"* India with its Soma, China and its mushrooms, Africa with iboga root, and South America with ayahuasca. These substances induce a spiritual experience, and shamans also use them as a tool for healing practices and accessing the spirit world. Furthermore, entheogens are thought to have been used by various cultures for thousands of years now.

Shamanistic practices often incorporate entheogens to connect with other realms. Entheogens are substances that cause an altered state of consciousness (ASC), allowing users to feel different than usual, including relaxed, excited, or energized. They can be plants, fungi, or artificial chemicals, such as:

- Psilocybin mushrooms and LSD
- Mescaline found in peyote cacti

- Ayahuasca made from the vine banisteriopsis caapi and psychotria viridis
- Fly agaric mushrooms (amanita muscaria)
- Morning glory seeds containing LSA (Lysergic Acid Amide)
- Hawaiian baby wood.

These substances can trigger intense spiritual experiences where users believe they have reached a higher level of being. Likewise, entheogens use has existed throughout history for various spiritual and medicinal purposes.

Indigenous groups worldwide have been utilizing entheogens in their spiritual practices for centuries. These psychoactive substances, such as iboga root bark and peyote cactus, have powerful mind-altering effects that can bring about profound changes in consciousness. Unlike psychedelics, which often lead to confusion and disorientation, entheogens impart peace and clarity. In shamanic rituals, they are said to enable shamans to traverse into other worlds or realms beyond this one, where they can communicate with divine entities. The psychedelic experience is commonly described as an exploration of the depths of one's psyche. At the same time, an entheogenic journey could be seen as a voyage beyond the self into another reality entirely. Entheogens are also known for promoting experiences of profound insight and healing.

Meanwhile, shamans use entheogens to bridge the gap between worlds, allowing them to connect with the spiritual realm. Entheogens range from naturally derived plants and mushrooms to synthetic compounds. The benefits of these substances can vary depending on their nature, dosage, and administration. For example, some may be used as healing agents, while others are used for divination or personal exploration. Ayahuasca, in particular, is one of the most potent entheogens and has been used in South American shamanic rituals for thousands of years to acquire spiritual knowledge or communicate with spirits. However, while psychotropic drugs such as LSD, cannabis, and magic mushrooms produce mind-altering effects, they may not induce a spiritual experience and access higher realms of consciousness.

Today's indigenous people still use entheogens, which have been used in shamanic rituals for thousands of years. While these substances can be dangerous if taken in excess or by those with pre-existing mental health conditions, they can also offer a spiritual experience that may help users connect with their identity as part of nature or humanity.

Conclusion

This book aims to provide an overview of the key aspects of shamanism, including its beliefs, practices, and techniques. I have delved into the rich and fascinating world of shamanic healing, spirit guides, and the three shamanic worlds. I also explored the role of dreams and trance in shamanic practice.

In restating the book's message, I have highlighted the importance of shamanism as an ancient spiritual practice that is still relevant and effective today. This practice is based on the notion that all things have a spirit or soul and are all interconnected in the universe. The shaman's role is to facilitate communication between the physical and spiritual realms, helping individuals heal and bring balance to their lives.

Shamanism is a spiritual practice that involves an altered state of consciousness, communicating with the spirit world and healing. It involves various techniques, such as drumming or chanting, to achieve an altered state of consciousness, which can be achieved through mind-expanding herbs or psychedelic plants. The goal of shamanism is to help people connect with their inner selves and access hidden knowledge, such as knowledge of past lives or future events. Shamans exist today, they are called healers, and they use similar techniques to traditional shamans.

The word shaman originates from the Tungusic languages, and it refers to a priest or healer who uses spiritual techniques to facilitate healing and communication with spirits. Traditional shamanism is based on direct experience, being an integral part of nature, and finding meaning through spiritual development. Modern-day shamanism is spiritual in nature, but it is not religion-based. In *The 4 Pillars of Shamanism*, I provide a comprehensive guide that explores these fundamental principles and practices in detail, offering insights and practical guidance for those seeking to deepen their understanding of shamanism and put its teachings into practice.

The first pillar of shamanism is a deep connection with the natural world. This connection is seen as the foundation of shamanic practice, and it is achieved through a deep respect and reverence for the natural world and its cycles and seasons. In this chapter, we explored how indigenous cultures have maintained this connection over the centuries and the practical steps that modern practitioners can take to deepen their connection with nature.

The second pillar of shamanism is the use of ritual and ceremony. In shamanic cultures, these rituals and ceremonies are seen as powerful tools for connecting with the spirit world and promoting healing and growth. In this chapter, we explored the different forms these rituals and ceremonies take and provided practical guidance on creating meaningful rituals and ceremonies.

The third pillar of shamanism is engagement with non-ordinary reality. This refers to the realm of the spirit world, which is seen as a parallel reality that is just as real as the physical world. In this chapter, we explored the different ways in which shamans engage with this realm, including the use of meditation, visualization, and other shamanic techniques. They also provide practical guidance on developing your own shamanic practices and engaging with the spirit world in meaningful ways.

Meanwhile, the fourth and final pillar of shamanism is the application of shamanic healing techniques. These techniques are used to promote physical, emotional, and spiritual healing, and they include practices such as the use of power animals, soul retrieval, and extraction. This chapter explored these techniques in detail and provided practical guidance for personal healing and growth.

Altogether, *The Four Pillars of Shamanism* presents a comprehensive overview of the ancient spiritual practice and its enduring relevance in today's world. By emphasizing the importance of the four pillars—connection to nature, community, spirituality, and healing—in fostering a holistic and fulfilling life, I make the book's message crystal clear.

Several essential aspects of shamanism, including shamanic healing and spirit guides, were also explored. Shamanic healing involves a shaman journeying to the spiritual realm to communicate with spirits and retrieve lost soul parts. Likewise, it restores balance and healing to the individual. This powerful healing form also addresses physical ailments and mental, emotional, relational, and financial issues. Alongside these practices, spirit guides from the spiritual realm provide guidance and support to the shaman as they journey towards greater spiritual understanding and personal growth. This book also touches on the unique teachings and qualities of the upper, middle, and lower worlds that the shaman can access during their transformative journeys.

Finally, we discussed the importance of dreams and trance in shamanic practice. Dreams provide a direct connection to the spiritual realm, and the shaman can use this connection to gain insights, guidance, and healing. Trance is a state of consciousness in which the shaman can access the spiritual realm and communicate with spirits; it is a crucial aspect of shamanic practice.

In delivering on my promise, this book has provided a comprehensive overview of the critical aspects of shamanism, illuminating this ancient spiritual practice's rich and fascinating world. Through its pages, I have aimed to shed light on the beliefs, practices, and techniques central to shamanism and provide a deeper understanding of this powerful and transformative path.

The book aims to help readers find harmony and balance in their lives by connecting with the spirit world through shamanism. Also, it provides a solution for those seeking a deeper understanding of shamanism and its benefits. Through clear and accessible language, I have guided you through the complexities of this spiritual tradition and shown how its principles and practices can be integrated into modern life.

The one thing you are meant to take away from this book is the understanding that shamanism offers a path to a more fulfilling and meaningful life. By embracing the four pillars of connection to nature, community, spirituality, and healing, individuals can cultivate a deeper sense of purpose and find greater peace and happiness daily. Whether one is seeking to explore shamanism for the first time or deepen their existing spiritual practice, *The 4 Pillars of Shamanism* provides a comprehensive and inspiring guide to this rich and ancient tradition.

Glossary

Altered State of Consciousness (ASC): A state of mind different from normal awareness and consciousness, typically characterized by changes in perception, thought, emotion, and memory.

Ancestors: The people from previous generations who have preceded you biologically or culturally.

Angels: Divine beings believed to act as messengers between the divine realm and the physical world, providing comfort, guidance, and protection to people.

Archangels: High-ranking angels in many religious traditions, often associated with specific qualities or duties, such as Michael as a protector or Gabriel as a messenger.

Aura: An energy field that is said to surround and permeate a person's body, often depicted as a colorful or luminous halo.

Breathing Exercises: Techniques used to regulate and control one's breathing, often as a form of meditation or stress relief.

Burnout: the loss of motivation and fulfillment brought on by a state of physical, emotional, and mental exhaustion brought on by excessive and prolonged stress or work.

Centering: A practice of bringing one's attention and focus to the present moment and the physical sensations in the body to reduce stress and increase awareness.

Ceremony: A formal and symbolic event, often religious or spiritual, performed to mark a significant occasion or bring people together.

Connecting: The process of creating a connection or relationship between two or more things.

Connection: A relationship or link between two or more things.

Crossing Over: A term used in many spiritual and religious traditions to describe a soul's transition from one plane of existence to another, such as from the physical world to the afterlife.

Cure: A treatment or solution that alleviates or eliminates an illness or condition.

Daily Practice: A routine or routine-like behavior performed regularly and repeatedly as a form of self-improvement or spiritual growth.

Deities: Divine or supernatural beings worshiped and revered in various religious and spiritual traditions, often associated with specific qualities, powers, or domains.

Delving Deeper: The act of exploring or investigating something more thoroughly or intensively, often to gain greater understanding or knowledge.

Despair: A feeling of hopelessness and despondency, often accompanied by loss or frustration from complex or challenging circumstances.

Diagnosis: An illness, disease, or condition's identification or determination of its nature and cause, typically made by a doctor or other medical professional.

Dimension: A direction or aspect along which a phenomenon or object can vary, or a concept in physics and mathematics that refers to a physical extent or a space-time coordinate.

Divination: The practice of seeking or revealing knowledge or guidance through supernatural means, such as interpreting omens, casting lots, or consulting oracles.

Divine: Of or relating to a deity or the divine, often associated with holiness, purity, and transcendence.

Divine Beings: Creatures or entities believed to be of a divine or supernatural origin or nature.

Divine Connection: A relationship or bond with the divine or spiritual realm, often experienced as a feeling of closeness or communication with a higher power.

Earth: The physical realm of existence and the natural world, including the elements of the land, water, air, fire, and spirit.

Earth Mother: A concept in many indigenous cultures that personifies the earth as a nurturing and sustaining mother, often associated with fertility, growth, and abundance.

Empath: A person with an enhanced capacity to perceive and comprehend the emotions and feelings of others.

Endorphins: Natural, feel-good chemicals the body produces to relieve pain and create a feeling of well-being.

Euphoria: A feeling of intense happiness, often accompanied by a sense of elation and excitement.

Evil Spirit: An entity some believe is a source of negative energy and influence in the world.

Exorcism: A ritual or practice to remove an evil spirit or negative entity from a person or place.

Guides: Spiritual beings, such as angels, are believed to guide and support individuals on their spiritual journey.

Healing: The procedure of regaining physical, mental, and spiritual balance.

Healing Methods: Various techniques are used to facilitate healing, such as meditation, visualization, Reiki, and acupuncture.

Healing Sessions: One-on-one sessions with a healer, during which the person receives guidance and support for their healing journey.

Heaven: A term used to describe a realm of existence believed by some to be a place of peace, happiness, and spiritual fulfillment.

Heavenly Beings: Spiritual entities believed by some to reside in Heaven and to offer guidance and support to individuals on Earth.

Hell: A term used to describe a realm of existence believed by some to be a place of suffering and punishment.

Helping Spirits: Spiritual entities believed by some to offer guidance and support to individuals on their spiritual journey.

Higher Power: A term used to describe a divine, spiritual force or entity believed to be greater than oneself.

Higher Realms of Understanding: Realms of existence believed by some to be beyond our physical world and to hold greater knowledge and wisdom.

Higher Self: A term used to describe the spiritual aspect of a person that is believed to be their true self beyond the physical body and ego.

Illness: A physical or mental condition that impairs normal functioning and well-being.

Incantations: Words or phrases repeated to achieve a specific outcome or influence a desired result.

Incense: A substance that produces a fragrant smoke when burned and is used in various spiritual practices for its symbolic or medicinal properties.

Innate Abilities: Natural talents or skills inherent in an individual without training or education.

Inner Guide: An intuition or inner voice thought to provide people on their spiritual journey with direction and wisdom.

Inner Self: A term used to describe the true self, beyond the physical body and ego, that is believed to hold inner wisdom and guidance.

Inner Voice: A voice or inner intuition thought to provide individuals with direction and wisdom along their spiritual path.

Inner Wisdom: A term used to describe an individual's internal knowledge and understanding that can be accessed through quiet reflection and introspection.

Integrating: The process of combining and integrating different aspects of oneself, such as the physical, emotional, mental, and spiritual aspects.

Intercession: A form of prayer where a person requests guidance from a higher power, for themselves or others.

Introspection: The process of looking within oneself and examining one's thoughts, feelings, and beliefs.

Intuition: An innate capacity to comprehend something intuitively and without using conscious thought.

Journeying: A spiritual or religious rite often performed on a physical journey.

Lost Soul Parts: Fragments of a person's soul essence that has become separated.

Magic Rituals: An event intended to bring about change in the world; a ceremony involving incantations, spells, and other rituals.

Manifestation: The process whereby an idea or image comes into being; the act of embodying something in visible form; the act of becoming apparent or visible.

Mantras: The repetition of a word or sound is known as a mantra, and it can be used to improve concentration, calm the mind, and promote relaxation.

Medicine Wheel: A medicine wheel is a sacred circle used in Native American ceremonies to symbolize the four elements and directions. Furthermore, it can be a helpful tool for vision quests and meditation.

Meditation: Meditation is an integral part of many religions and spiritual practices. It involves focusing on one thing for an extended period, usually, 10 minutes, to promote relaxation, clarity, and well-being.

Message Bearers: In Native American tradition, messengers from other worlds come to earth to teach us about ourselves and our place in the universe by sharing their wisdom through stories or songs. In some cultures, these messengers are called "spirit guides" or "guardians."

Metaphysical Level: The metaphysical level refers to ideas about spirituality—beliefs about what happens after death; whether we have souls; how we connect with God; etc.—as opposed to religious beliefs like which church you go to or what ceremonies you practice (those would be on the physical level).

Mindfulness: Mindfulness is a way of paying attention that focuses on being present in your life. Mindfulness can help you be more aware of your thoughts and feelings without judging them, which may reduce stress and improve your mental health.

Modern-Day Shamanism: A contemporary form of spiritual but not religion-based shamanism. It involves using your senses to interact with your environment, finding ways to connect with others, and working with energy to help heal yourself and others.

Mystics: Mystics are people who have a strong relationship with their spiritual beliefs and seek to understand their life experiences in those terms. They often seek out others interested in exploring these ideas and are surrounded by like-minded individuals.

Occult Traditions: Occult traditions are practices that involve the supernatural or paranormal. Depending on the intent of the person using it, the occult can be used for good or evil.

Omens: An omen is an event believed to foretell future events. Omens are usually associated with a spiritual belief system and occur randomly.

Painful Experiences: Some shamanic practices may require you to participate in painful or uncomfortable activities, such as fasting or exercise, to get in touch with your body's energy centers and bring positive energy into your life.

Pilgrimage. A journey undertaken for religious or spiritual reasons.

Pillars of Shamanism: The pillars of shamanism include: *spirit communication, healing work, trance work, journeying/dreaming, and ritual ceremony/drumming.* These pillars are used together to create a holistic approach towards life balance and healing work within yourself or others needing assistance from someone trained in this healing modality.

Power Animal: An animal spirit that serves as a guide and ally.

Power Animal Retrieval: A technique where the shamanic healer retrieves a person's power animal that has separated from them.

Power Retrieval: A shamanic practice of regaining one's lost personal power or life force.

Precognition: The ability to perceive or know events or information about the future through extrasensory means.

Primordial Deity: A deity believed to exist from the beginning of time and represents the elemental forces of the universe.

Psychedelic Plants/Mushrooms: Plants or mushrooms that can induce an altered state of mind.

Psychic healing: A type of healing that involves using psychic or spiritual energy to help balance and align the individual's energy field and promote physical, mental, and emotional well-being.

Psychopomp: A being, deity, or entity that guides the souls of the deceased to the afterlife.

Psychotherapy: A form of therapy that aims to treat mental disorders by altering a patient's thoughts and behaviors.

Rattle: A musical instrument typically made of a handle and a container filled with small objects that produce a sound when shaken. It is used in various spiritual and religious practices, including shamanism.

Rattling: Shaking a rattle in a spiritual or religious context to produce sound and create specific energy.

Real Beings: Beings or entities that exist physically or spiritually and can be perceived through the senses or extrasensory means.

Realities: Different dimensions, realms, or realities that exist beyond our physical reality and can be accessed through spiritual practices or experiences.

Realms of Reality: Different levels or domains of existence beyond our physical reality can be experienced through spiritual or supernatural means.

Reflection: The act of considering or examining one's thoughts, emotions, and actions to gain insight and understanding.

Ritualized Practices: Practices or activities that have been formalized or structured as part of a spiritual or religious tradition.

Rituals: A set of actions or words performed in a specific way, often as part of a spiritual or religious tradition.

Scandinavian: Relating to the countries of Scandinavia (Norway, Sweden, and Denmark), their cultures, and their people.

Scent: A particular smell, especially a pleasant one.

Scrying: A divination technique that involves using a reflective surface, such as a crystal ball, to see visions or receive information from the spiritual realm.

Shaman: A spiritual practitioner who uses altered states of consciousness to access the spirit world and bring back information and healing to the community.

Shamanic Healing: A type of healing that involves working with spirits, energies, and elements of nature to promote physical, mental, and emotional well-being.

Shamanic Journey: A spiritual journey or meditation where a shaman accesses the spirit world to gain insight, healing, or knowledge.

Shamanic Journeying: The practice of accessing the spirit world through a journey or meditation, often guided by a shaman or a spiritual teacher.

Shamanic Practices: Techniques used in shamanism, such as drumming, chanting, or psychedelics, to achieve an ASC.

Shamanic Worlds: The worlds that shamans travel to interact with the spirits.

Shamanism: is a form of spiritual practice in which a person called a shaman enters an altered state of consciousness to communicate with and heal others.

Shape-Shifting: When someone takes on the physical characteristics of something else.

Signs: Things that represent something else, like a signpost or symbol.

Sky Deity: The deity who lives in or rules over the sky.

Soul: The eternal part of you and the force that breathes life into your body; it is composed of your positive traits and life experiences, which influence your decisions.

Soul Flight: When you leave your body into another world or state of being, like in astral projection.

Soul Growth: What happens during soul flight; is growth, development, and learning about yourself and others.

Soul Retrieval: A shamanic ritual in which a lost soul is rescued and returned safely home.

Spirit: The force that exists outside of time and space. It comprises other people's souls, animals and plants, planets, stars, and other things outside the human experience.

Spirit Allies: People or animals who have chosen to support you on your life's journey. They can appear in dreams or visions as guides or guardians.

Spirit Communication: Talking with spirits using meditation, divination tools like tarot cards or pendulums, or other methods such as channeling (which involves speaking through another person).

Spirit Guides: People who have died but still have a presence in our world; they are usually referred to as ancestors or angels in Western culture (though the definition of each varies). They are often considered intermediaries for communicating with the spirit world.

Spiritual Development: A journey towards a higher level of consciousness. It is the process by which one's awareness expands and becomes more universal. Spiritual development is achieved through meditation, yoga, prayer, and other spiritual practices.

Spiritual Guide: A person who assists another individual in their spiritual development.

Spiritual Leader: The person who leads a community or religious group; a religious leader, an inspirational figure, or simply someone who teaches others how to live more spiritually.

Spiritual Path: A path that one chooses to follow to achieve enlightenment or union with God through meditation, yoga, prayer, and other spiritual practices.

Spiritual Realm: A realm of existence outside the physical world where spirits dwell and angels are believed to reside; also known as heaven.

Stamina: The ability to continue doing something over an extended period without tiring easily; perseverance; strength of will.

Supernatural World: A nonconventional world that defies physics and scientific laws.

Sweat Lodge Ceremony: A purification ceremony that promotes physical, emotional, and spiritual healing.

Synchronicity: A phrase that describes encountering coincidences that defy logic.

The Spirit World: A place where all souls go after death; it can be accessed through meditation or other spiritual practices such as astral projection (which involves leaving one's body behind temporarily).

Trance: A state of being where you are so focused on something that you are unaware of your surroundings.

Trance State: A state in which a person becomes absorbed with an activity or idea and is withdrawn from others or their surroundings.

Visions: Seeing something that is not there, usually through drugs or meditation.

Water Spirits: Spirits that live in water, such as lakes, rivers, or oceans.

References

Aletheia. (2018, February 5). *7 types of spirit guides (& how to connect with them).* LonerWolf. https://lonerwolf.com/spirit-guides/

Bernstein, G. (2020, February 28). *10 simple and beautiful ways to connect with your spirit guides.* Gabby Bernstein. https://gabbybernstein.com/spirit-guides/

Dreaming research papers - 894 words | Bartleby. (n.d.). Www.bartleby.com. https://www.bartleby.com/essay/Dreaming-Research-Papers-FJAF9CC44EV

Faria, M. (2021, July 12). *"Plants of the gods" and their hallucinogenic powers in neuropharmacology — A review of two books.* Surgical Neurology International. https://doi.org/10.25259/sni_560_2021

Farmer, S. D. (n.d.). *Signs from the animal world.* Unity.org. https://www.unity.org/article/signs-animal-world

Halliday, M. (n.d.). *Introduction to the medicine wheel | The Edinburgh Shamanic Centre.* Www.shamaniccentre.com. https://www.shamaniccentre.com/teachings-medicinewheel.html

Harner, M. (n.d.). *A core shamanic theory of dreams.* https://www.shamanism.org/articles/pdfs/ShamanicTheoryDreams3-11.pdf

Harner, M. (2005). *Articles on shamanism and shamanic studies: my path in shamanism by Michael Harner, from higher wisdom by Roger Walsh and Charles S. Grob*. Www.shamanism.org. https://www.shamanism.org/articles/article16page4.html

https://hraf.yale.edu/author/ajordan. (2019, March 27). *cross-culturally exploring the concept of shamanism*. Human Relations Area Files - Cultural Information for Education and Research. https://hraf.yale.edu/cross-culturally-exploring-the-concept-of-shamanism/

Jackson, J. (2018, August 15). *Shamanism - spiritual guides for indigenous peoples*. Www.linkedin.com. https://www.linkedin.com/pulse/shamanism-spiritual-guides-indigenous-peoples-julian-jackson/

Kapoor, M. (2022, December 29). *5 certain signs that your higher self is talking to you*. Mukund Kapoor's Blog. https://mukundkapoor.com/signs-that-your-higher-self-is-talking-to-you

Labate, B., Laboa, B., Mizumoto, S., Anderson, B., & Cavnar, C. (2014). The therapeutic use of ayahuasca. In *www.academia.edu*. https://www.academia.edu/27695463/The_therapeutic_use_of_ayahuasca

Mazzola, L. C. (1988). The Medicine Wheel: Center and Periphery. *The Journal of Popular Culture*, *22*(2), 63–73. https://doi.org/10.1111/j.0022-3840.1988.2202_63.x

McClenon, J. (1997). Shamanic Healing, Human Evolution, and the Origin of Religion. *Journal for the Scientific Study of Religion*, *36*(3), 345. https://doi.org/10.2307/1387852

McNamara, P., & Bulkeley, K. (2015). Dreams as a source of supernatural agent concepts. *Frontiers in Psychology, 6*. https://doi.org/10.3389/fpsyg.2015.00283

Metzner, R. (2013). Entheogenic rituals, shamanism and green psychology. *European Journal of Ecopsychology, 4*, 64–77. https://citeseerx.ist.psu.edu/document?repid=rep1&type=pdf&doi=284ee8a0cbefa64d1d28a98eaffc975c9863819a

Louie, M. (n.d.). *Shaman*. Michele Louie Awakening the Healer Within. https://michelelouie.com/shaman/

Oracle, L. (n.d.). *Luminous oracle*. Luminous Oracle. https://luminousoracle.com/

Plant spirit shamanism: working with plant medicine in shamanic journeys. (2022, April 27). Therapeutic Shamanism. https://www.therapeutic-shamanism.co.uk/blog/plant-medicine/

Plants of mind and spirit. (n.d.). Www.fs.usda.gov. https://www.fs.usda.gov/wildflowers/ethnobotany/Mind_and_Spirit/index.shtml

Filippo, D. S. (2006). *Angels as spiritual guides*. National Louis University Digital Commons @ NLU. https://digitalcommons.nl.edu/cgi/viewcontent.cgi?article=1054&context=faculty_publications

Shamanic healing. (n.d.). I.e. KAWA. https://www.iekawa.com/soulsessions

Shamanic journeying / psycho shamanic. (n.d.). Www.goodtherapy.org. https://www.goodtherapy.org/learn-about-therapy/types/shamanic-journeying-psycho-shamanic

Shamanism - selection. (n.d.). Encyclopedia Britannica. https://www.britannica.com/topic/shamanism/Selection

Shamanistic healing - 2028 words. (n.d.). Www.123helpme.com. https://www.123helpme.com/essay/Shamanistic-Healing-30632

Shamans. (n.d.). Nordan.daynal.org. https://nordan.daynal.org/wiki/Shamans

Thomason, T. C. (n.d.). *The role of altered states of consciousness in Native American healing.* Ecstatic Trance: Ritual Body Postures. https://www.cuyamungueinstitute.com/articles-and-news/the-role-of-altered-states-of-consciousness-in-native-american-healing/

University of Minnesota. (2006). *Shamanism.* Taking Charge of Your Health & Wellbeing. https://www.takingcharge.csh.umn.edu/shamanism

What is shamanic healing? (n.d.). Www.centreofexcellence.com. https://www.centreofexcellence.com/shamanic-healing/#:~:text=Also%20known%20as%20a%20

Williams, K. (2022). *What is a shaman? types, talents & examples.* Study.com. https://study.com/learn/lesson/what-is-a-shaman.html

Printed in Great Britain
by Amazon

45160917R00079